March 1989

My dear Bennett,

Welcome Home!

Love always,
Armin

THE ENCYCLOPEDIA OF ORNAMENT

THE ENCYCLOPEDIA OF ORNAMENT

A. RACINET

PORTLAND HOUSE
NEW YORK

The Encyclopedia of Ornament
was originally published in 1873
by Henry Sotheran and Co., London,
under the title *Polychromatic Ornament.*

This 1988 edition published by Portland House,
a division of dilithium Press, Ltd., distributed
by Crown Publishers, Inc., 225 Park Avenue South,
New York, New York 10003.

Printed and bound in Hong Kong.

ISBN 0-517-66297-3

h g f e d c b a

TABLE OF CONTENTS.

LIST OF PLATES

IN THE ORDER IN WHICH THEY ARE ARRANGED, WITH THE NAMES OF THE SYMBOLS

BY WHICH THEY ARE DISTINGUISHED.

CLASSIFIED LIST OF THE SUBJECTS CONTAINED

IN THE PLATES.

WOVEN FABRICS.

Stuffs, Tapestries, Embroideries, and Printed Cloth.

RIMITIVE; Plate I. Chinese and Japanese; Plates XIII., XIV., and XV. Indian; Plates XVIII. and XIX. Persian; Plates XX., XXIII., and XXV. Byzantine; Plate XXXV. Middle Ages; Plates XLI. and XLVII. Renaissance; Plate LXXIII. Seventeenth and eighteenth centuries; Plates LXXVIII., LXXXIII., LXXXV., LXXXVII., LXXXVIII., LXXXIX., XCII., XCV., and XCVII.

LEATHER AND BINDINGS.

Arabian; Plate XXVI. Renaissance; Plates LXVIII. and LXIX. Seventeenth and eighteenth centuries; Plates LXXV., LXXVIII., LXXXV., LXXXVI., and XCII.

KERAMICS.

Terra-Cotta, painted, glazed, and enamelled; Earthenware and Porcelain; Decorations of Utensils;
Pavements and Wall-Facings.

Assyrian; Plate IV. Greek; Plates V. and VI. Indian; Plate XIX. Persian; Plate XXII. Moorish; Plate XXIX. Middle Ages; Plate XLVI. Renaissance; Plates LIX., LX., and LXVII. Seventeenth and eighteenth centuries; Plates LXXXII. and XCVIII.

MOSAICS.

Greek; Plate VI. Greco-Roman; Plate IX. Moorish; Plate XXIX. Byzantine; Plates XXXI., XXXIII., XXXV., XXXVI., and XXXVII. Seventeenth century; Plate LXXXI.

INCRUSTATIONS AND NIELLOS.

Chinese; Plate X. Indian; Plates XVI., XVII., and XVIII. Persian; Plate XXI. Renaissance; Plates LVI. and LXVIII. Seventeenth and eighteenth centuries; Plates LXXIV., LXXVIII., and LXXXIV.

GOLDSMITH'S WORK AND JEWELLERY.

Cloisonné and other Enamels; Gold Enamel; Jewellery; Chasing.

Egyptian; Plate III. Assyrian; Plate IV. Etruscan; Plate VII. Chinese and Japanese; Plates XI. and XII. Indian; Plate XIX. Byzantine; Plate XXXV. Middle Ages; Plates XLI. and XLIX. Renaissance; Plates LIX., LXII., and LXIV. Seventeenth and eighteenth centuries; Plates LXXIV., LXXVI., XCIV., and XCVI.

PAINTINGS ON MANUSCRIPTS.

Primitive (Mexican); Plate I. Indian; Plate XVIII. Persian; Plate XXIV. Arabian; Plates XXVII. and XXVIII. Byzantine; Plates XXXI., XXXII., XXXIII., and XXXIV. Celtic; Plates XXXVIII. and XXXIX. Middle Ages; Plates XL., XLI., XLII., XLIII., XLVIII., XLIX., L., and LI. Renaissance; Plates LII., LV., LVII., LXI., LXIII., LXIV., LXVI., and LXX. Seventeenth century; Plate LXXVI.

FRESCOES.

Sculptures in Bas-relief; Paintings on Glass.

Egyptian; Plates II. and III. Assyrian; Plate IV. Greek; Plate VI. Greco-Roman; Plates VIII. and IX. Moorish; Plate XXX. Byzantine; Plate XXXI. Middle Ages; Plates XLI., XLIV., and XLV. Renaissance; Plates LIII., LIV., and LXVI. Seventeenth and eighteenth centuries; Plates LXXIV., LXXVI., LXXIX., LXXX., LXXXI., XC., XCIX., and C.

PAINTED WOOD.

Primitive; Plate I. Indian; Plates XVII. and XIX. Renaissance; Plate LXV. Seventeenth and eighteenth centuries; Plates LXXIV., XCI., XCII. and XCIX.

CARTOUCHES.

Egyptian; Plate II., No. 12, Plate III., No. 1. Chinese; Plate XI., Nos. 18, and 19; and Plate XIII. Persian; Plate XXI., No. 15; Plates XXIV. and XXV. Arabian; Plates XXVI., XXVII., and XXVIII. Renaissance, seventeenth and eighteenth centuries; Plates comprising cartouches only; LVIII., LXXI., LXXII., LXXVII., and XCIII.; other plates containing specimens, LII., LIV., LVI., LVII., LIX., LX., LXI., LXIII., LXVII., LXIX., LXX., LXXIX., LXXX., LXXXI., LXXXIII., LXXXVI., XCI., XCIV., XCVI., and XCVIII.

INTRODUCTION.

HIS book is meant to be chiefly practical, being less a treatise than a collection, and teaching more by example than by precept. By the adoption of this method we have avoided the discussion of dangerous theories, which, however correct they may be, remain too vague and general when presented in an abstract manner. Nothing can be more eloquent than the sight of the master-pieces themselves; and to point out by analysis the lessons they contain is a proceeding much more conclusive than to pretend to demonstrate them by an *à priori* synthesis, frequently too absolute to be adapted to the many unavoidable exceptions, or the necessities of peculiar cases. The latter method would be especially dangerous if applied to that branch of art which is least capable of adapting itself to inflexible laws, and in which the greatest liberty has to be left to the instinct, the imagination, or even to the caprice of the artist.

Most assuredly, however, we would not say that the productions of this art can dispense with obedience to certain principles and superior laws, to which every artistic conception must conform.

Thus, an ornamental composition can only be perfectly beautiful when it produces in the spectator that sentiment of repose and satisfaction which results from the equilibrium and perfect harmony of the elements of which it is composed. The laws of proportion, the laws of balancing and symmetry, the subordination of details to the whole, variety in unity, all these rules, dictated by instinct and proclaimed by science, are binding on the art of ornamentation as on all others.

But yet, whilst painting and sculpture are more or less fettered by sense and logic, or by the necessity of the imitation and exact rendering of natural objects; whilst architecture must comply with various conditions—solidity, the purpose of the building, and the correlation of exterior aspect with interior use; ornament, and especially that kind which now occupies us—the decoration of coloured surfaces—has a sphere of action, doubtless more modest, but yet enjoying much greater liberty.

Many means exist by which this end may be attained, many ways of arriving at this combination of proportion and harmony which gives birth to the sentiment of the beautiful.

If ornament may borrow from other arts their various characteristics—from architecture its general forms and the interest attaching to repetitions and variations of the same motive; from sculpture its real or imitated reliefs; from painting the charms of episodic subjects and of natural colouring—it may, without diverging from its proper sphere, find inexhaustible resources.

From the simplest geometric figure—a square, a lozenge, or a triangle, the repetition and intermingling of which frequently suffice to form an interesting whole—to the most ingeniously complicated interlacings, the most capricious arabesques, and those chimerical compositions in which the line, the flower, the animal and the human figure are mixed and blended together, what a vast domain for the ornamentalist, who thus finds himself master of that fantastic and charming world, which depends not on nature but on the imagination! What captivating and even seductive liberty, if such freely-ranging caprice were not to be regulated by taste and judged by the effect produced, which must be, whatever the means employed, harmony in form as well as in colour!

Thus, the place which ornament occupies in the artistic scale is, though a secondary yet an important one. If it is less ambitious than other forms of art, if it does not attempt like them to raise our souls and make them vibrate with the deepest feelings, it responds to one of the most instinctive needs of our nature, that of embellishing the objects around us.

Sometimes united to the creations of the higher arts in order to complete them, sometimes applied to the commonest objects, which it relieves and ennobles, it is the natural link between industry and art, of which it represents one of the most familiar, practical, and varied forms.

Thus the general characteristics of ornamentation are a multiplicity of applications, and an almost unlimited variety and liberty in the employment of means. But from this very character there arises, as we said just now, a great difficulty in determining its rules otherwise than by example, and in forming *à priori* the *Code of Ornament*.

This, then, we have not attempted, and it is solely by analysis and by considering in their historical order the various styles from which the subjects of our plates are taken, that we shall endeavour, in this short introduction, to explain their sources and mechanism, and to furnish those who will make use of it with the means of enlightened appreciation and imitation, or what is better, of profitable appropriation. With this view before us, we shall only preface this historical sketch by a few brief preliminary observations calculated to lighten the way and provide the elements for a conclusion which the reader can draw for himself.

There are three processes in the production of ornament—the *drawing* or *design, colouring,* and *relief.*

By the help of these means, the two first of which are especially to occupy our attention, the artist may obtain the most varied results, all coming, however, within the three following categories:

1st. The *invention* of subjects purely imaginary, foreign to the productions of nature.

2ndly. The *conventional representation* of natural objects, expressed merely in their essential characters, and under generalized types.

3rdly. The *imitative representation* of objects, in which nature is followed both as regards design and colouring.

The first, which borrows nothing from the imitative arts, appears to a certain degree in every style and in every period. The lineal and geometric combinations (interlacings, meanders, and roses), which are its primitive basis, respond to the faculties of order and measure which are to be found in every human brain; being the direct productions of pure imagination, they create that which had no existence. Although this style occupies a more important place in the art of certain nations, such as the Arabs or Anglo-Saxons, yet in none is it wholly wanting. Whether apparent or not, this geometric process forms the basis of the greater number of ornamental compositions.

The second, the *conventional* representation, which is a link between the two others and is frequently mixed with the first, resembles this first style to some degree in the domain of creative invention, by its faculty of idealizing, that is, of generalizing under the form of archetypes, and of appropriating the models taken from nature. It is by this idealized imitation, that the artist, according to the happy expression of M. Charles Blanc, " enters into the grandeur of universal life;" and it is from this style that we may expect the highest type of ornament; since, as the author of the " *Grammaire des Arts du Dessin*" says again, " this style is the impress of the human mind on nature."

As to the purely *imitative* representation of objects, it is when approaching modern times that we most frequently meet with this individualizing style, the especial aim of which is to give the most exact rendering of the object represented, to express it with all its accidental modifications, reliefs, and shades of colour; in short, with all its distinctive qualities and complete physiognomy. This style, the results of which are less severe and more delicate than those of the two others, arose from the increased use of painting in the domestic arts, and the improvement in the manual skill of the artist, and was thus well suited to the refined and elegant tastes of an advanced civilization. This frequent use of purely imitative painting suggested charming decorations to the skilful artists who adorned modern art, especially that of France, in the seventeenth and eighteenth centuries; not, however, altogether without abuse as well as injury to certain industrial arts (such as keramics, painting on glass, the manufacture of carpets, &c.), which would have gained by keeping to, and would even now gain by returning to, simpler and more truly decorative processes.

We will only say in conclusion that the application of colour to ornament (the principal object of this work) is bound up in the closest manner with the use of one or other of the modes of proceeding we have just explained. Where the representation of objects is ideal or conventional, the colour is likewise conventional, and the ornamentalist remains master of his palette. The severity of the design is thus redeemed by liberty in chromatics, that is to say, by the advantage of being able to choose and arrange the colours at will, without any necessity for resemblance or even for probability, but merely observing the laws of harmony. This road, always open to creative originality, was never abandoned by the Orientals, and in following it they acquired unequalled experience.

We will now trace, through the history of the different periods of art, the application of the various styles, the substance of which we have endeavoured to define.

PRIMITIVE DECORATION.

PLATE I.

AMONG the examples contained in Plate 1, the term *primitive*, that is to say anterior to any conception of rules of art, belongs in reality only to those examples (Nos. 1 to 17), which represent the almost instinctive conceptions of the tribes of Oceania or Central Africa, applied to the decoration of objects in common use. We have thought it advisable to add to this succinct glance at instinctive ornamentation, a few monochromatic fragments, carved or sculptured, which serve to complete its simple characteristics.

 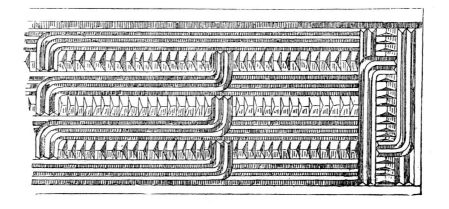

Fragments of Carving (Louvre Museum).

Except in Nos. 4, 8, and 12 of our plate, in which some outlines of flowers are to be found, all these instinctive designs are pure creations. The extremely moderate use of colour, he abuse of which is so easy, is no less remarkable than the manner of the design. Considered as primitive, this stage of art is not without its value, since, in the absence of a knowledge of higher rules, the workman would feel strongly at the very outset the need of order, symmetry, and harmony, his combinations being limited, it is true, but already characterized by appropriate colouring. Nowhere shall we find a more vigorous use of black than may be seen in Nos. 2 and 10, and especially in No. 4, where, on a bright red ground, the isolating principle of the white outline gives that powerful aid to effect so frequently obtained by the subtle colourists of Asia.

To these productions, presenting every characteristic of primitive art, we have added several examples of Peruvian or Mexican ornamentation belonging to a more advanced stage of civilization. We have done this because, in the first place, the limits of our collection do not allow us to give a separate place to those little-known arts, and also because it seemed to us interesting to place together, so as to mark the difference between, the purely individual efforts, such as those of wild tribes, and those in which the influence of architecture, in procuring unity of character, may already be felt.

Certainly the Mexican paintings given under Nos. 22 to 47 are not of an agreeable colouring, but beneath the barbarism of colour the intentions are not without value, and flow from the high principles, whence flow the different styles; principles to which architecture alone gave birth, and of which the ancient monuments of Yucatan and Mexico, reminding us of those of Egypt, India, Japan, and especially of Assyria, furnish prototypes.

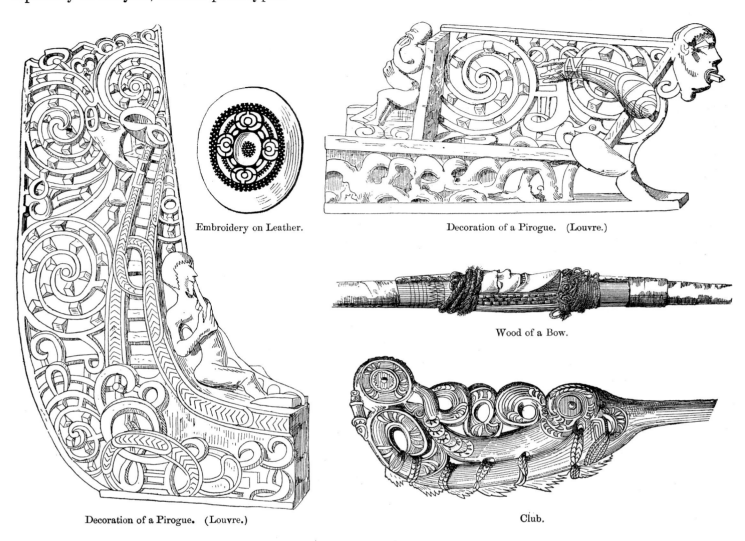

Embroidery on Leather.

Decoration of a Pirogue. (Louvre.)

Wood of a Bow.

Decoration of a Pirogue. (Louvre.)

Club.

Between the primitive state, and the establishment of architectural rules, it may easily be seen that a period of gestation must have elapsed, which we have no means of measuring or of following.

Authentic history does not even commence for us with the oldest monuments of architecture; we know

Braided Leather. (Modern Mexican Decoration. Louvre.)

nothing of the civilizations which erected them, and what may remain of preceding ages is still of no utility to us. " In the state of intermixture in which the great human families are now found spreading over the surface of the globe," says M. Viollet-le-Duc (" *Cités et Ruines Américaines* "), " it is difficult to distinguish the particular aptitudes which originally belonged to each of them." This is unfortunately evident, but yet we may, with Ziegler, and without entering into the pre-historic study of particular aptitudes, consider

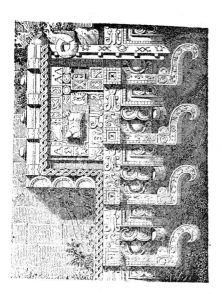

Pieces of the Monuments of Uxmal (Yucatan).
Taken from " *Monuments anciens et modernes* " by Gailhabaud; Paris, Firmin Didot.

keramics as the element which inspired the formula of architectural design. The analogy between the principles is the same, and man handled the potter's clay before the wood or stone of monuments. It is to keramics then that we must attribute the fertile principles of the idealization and generalization of the forms of nature from which architecture and ornamentation were to derive such great advantages.

ANCIENT ART.

IN classing under this denomination Egyptian, Assyrian, Greek, Etruscan, Roman, and Greco-Roman art, we are influenced less by a question of priority (since Asiatic art co-existed with that of later times, while some of its forms may claim the highest imaginable antiquity,) than by deference for the time-honoured phraseology which reserves this term *ancient* for those states of civilization which were made known to us by Greek and Latin literature, and the study of which, brought into honour at the time of the Renaissance, forms the principal basis of our classical education.

This group has besides a well-defined physiognomy which favours its study by itself, and its tradition may be easily followed through the various historical phases which these nations have passed through.

EGYPTIAN AND ASSYRIAN.

PLATES II., III.

Egyptian.

THE history of ancient art commences in Egypt.
Whether the arts of ancient Egypt be considered as a point of junction of the Semitic, Ethiopian, and Berber races, as a summing up of the attempts of earlier civilizations which have remained almost unknown to us, or be looked at as the origin of the Greek, Etruscan and Greco-Roman arts, that is to say, as the source of classical traditions, they have a two-fold claim to our respect in their antiquity and superior merits.

The art of the Egyptians was essentially lofty, spiritualistic and symbolic, and this character is to be found in the highest degree in their ornamental compositions.

The elements of the real world, combined under generalized forms, compose the basis of their decoration. The sober outlines within which it is contained are of unequalled amplitude; their only object is the expression of the species, not of the individual, and they represent, under ideal forms, types, which, though few, are very varied in their application.

The colouring consists of flat tints, without shading, employed in a conventional manner like the forms themselves. In the notice on Plate II. there will be found an enumeration of the colours used on the Egyptian's palette.

Nearly all the objects which compose this ornamentation are plainly symbols.

M. Jacquemart, in his "*Merveilles de la céramique,*" thus explains the greater part of the images represented in our two plates :—

" It is easy to show the important part played by a plant which is to be found in all Oriental theories. The deified lotus represents the homage rendered to the beneficent action of water and sun on the sleeping earth ; it is the symbolism of the annual evolutions of the seasons, causing generation to succeed generation, and bringing back life where every thing seemed like the immobility of death. The sun itself was the object of direct worship, the forms of which were varied by the priests to make it penetrate more deeply among the masses. Everyone is familiar with the winged disc, under which the two serpents Uræus raise their heads, the royal symbols of Upper and Lower Egypt ; it is the sun in his material form as he figures on the threshold of the temples, on the funereal and votive monuments, and even on the clothing of the priests and kings ; ardent and poetic prayers were addressed to it, such as the following :—' Glory to thee, Ra, in thy morning radiance, Tmon, in thy setting. . . . . Thou dost illumine, thou dost shine, appearing as the sovereign of the gods." But there is another solar image which demands an explanation. In the country, in our own land, we find an insect generally looked at with disgust, the beetle . . . Now, if the Egyptians chose out for deification such a small and repulsive being, it was because they had discovered wonderful details in its habits. And, indeed, when we observe the actions of this insect on sandy slopes, we see it penetrate into animal excrements, choose a suitable mass which it kneads into a ball, after having placed its egg within, and which it afterwards drags along by its hind legs, until the heat has hardened the surface ; it then buries the ball, in the interior of which the birth and transformation of the larva are to take place, and from which will afterwards emerge the perfect insect, to accomplish in its turn all the various processes of generation. The scarabæus appeared then to the Egyptians to be imitating, on a small scale, the work of the Creator. The stercoraceous ball, containing an egg, is the ground animated with the vital germ and undergoing, under the influence of solar heat, its natural evolution. Here there is some resemblance between the Creator and the work produced, and this resemblance sufficed to raise the humble insect to the rank of the greatest of gods."

No. 12 in Plate II. represents the black scarabæus holding in its upper claws the sun's disc, and in the lower ones the stercoraceous ball. It is the complete symbol.

To these symbolic representations, the Egyptians frequently added hieroglyphic signs. Writing thus became to them a means of ornament, a process which the Greeks appear to have neglected, but from which the Persians, Arabs and Moors obtained the happiest effects.

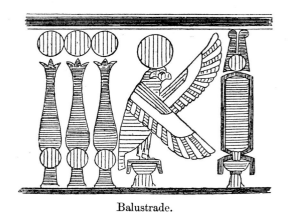

Balustrade.

Egyptian feather.

The following passage from M. Champollion-Figeac will give an idea of the extent of the application of ornament amongst the Egyptians :—

" Furniture of common or of rare and exotic woods, of metals either engraved or decorated with gilding ; plain and figured stuffs, embroidered, dyed and painted, of linen, cotton and silk, all contributed to the adornment of Egyptian houses, and to the convenience of home life . . . . The same care was given to the fabrication of steps, bedsteads with head-boards and bolsters, divans, sofas, wardrobes with two doors, sideboards, small tables, caskets and chests, and everything of that kind necessary for the use of a family. The footstool matched in material and ornaments with the arm-chair for which it was intended. There were folding-seats in wood, the legs having the form of the head and neck of a swan. Other arm-chairs were made of cedar-wood incrusted with ivory and ebony, and the seats of cane firmly interwoven. Stands, round tables, gaming-tables, boxes of all sizes corresponded in material and workmanship with the remainder of the furniture. Mats and carpets of brilliant and varied colours and sometimes adorned with pictures illustrating stories, covered the floor of the apartment or those portions of it that were most used : in the rooms there were also vases of gold, of costly materials, of gilded metals, relieved with enamels and precious stones, of an elegance and variety of form, of which we should have had no idea but for the paintings of them which remain."

The firmness, justness and fulness of the Egyptian drawing have never been surpassed. The lines of their hieroglyphics covering the papyrus and the stela, and executed in running hand, surpass sometimes in representations of animals even the finest works of the Greeks. The fact of these good draughtsmen restraining motion in their pictures into what appears to us extreme rigidity, showed a purpose that cannot be attributed to their religious laws alone. In resisting the pliability of their skilful and learned hand, they were obeying principles of art, of which they proved the fertility and which deserve on that account all our attention. The study of Egyptian productions is full of instruction, first as to what they are in themselves, and secondly, as to what they did not wish to be. Their sober outlines, whether simple lineaments or metallic envelopes, constantly remain before us as models for those ornamentalists who wish to retain the conditions of idealism and grandeur of style.

Assyrian.—Assyrian ornamentation, fragments of which are given in Plate IV., belongs to a secondary period, and might be called, as we remarked in our notice, the Scytho-Assyrian; it is indeed posterior to the conquest of primitive Babylon, whose arts must have come from that Indo-Bactrian source, still represented in Iran by monuments of which we possess no detailed drawings.

The Egyptian influence is seen clearly in some parts of the buildings of Persepolis: the winged globe, the head-dress of the Egyptian divinity Socharis, Uræus and balusters surmounted by the globe, prove that these buildings, enriched with borrowed ornaments, are posterior to the conquest of Egypt by Cambyses. No rule, no prescription of any school, seems to oppose the variety of forms, in which there is greater caprice than just proportion. We feel that the Egyptian artists summoned by the successors of Cambyses lost some of their worth when leaving the place of their education, which was already itself in a relative state of decay, and that they succeeded but imperfectly in transplanting their art to another land. Having to apply itself on a new soil to the decoration of palaces and no longer of temples, Egyptian symbolism no longer possesses the same hieratic meaning; brought face to face with a foreign civilization, there remain but feeble vestiges of it. No. 1 in our plate is a painted bas-relief representing the sacred tree, one of the most frequently repeated figures in Assyrian symbolism. The winged figures surrounding the sun, No. 2, seem to be the symbol of the soul, &c.

Assyrian ornamentation, including the bas-reliefs, was entirely painted, or gilded and silvered. "I have ascertained," says M. Texier, when speaking of Persepolis, "that there is not a corner of the palace in which there is not the most delicate and careful painting; it was the same at Khorsabad, at Nimroud, and also at Ecbatana, the capital of Media, where, according to Polybius, in his description of the palace of the kings of Persia, the porticoes, the peristyles, the walls were covered with plates of gold and silver, which were pillaged by the soldiers of Alexander."

The enamelled bricks of regular design and overlapping, of which we give two fine specimens, must be, from their manufacture, a Chinese importation (Texier, *Asie-Mineure*); at any rate, they are the earliest models of the bricks for facings, of which the modern Persians make so large and ingenious a use.

GREEK, ETRUSCAN, AND GRECO-ROMAN.

Plates V., VI.

Greek.

GREEK art in its commencement is thought to have been merely a continuation of the Egyptian tradition, modified by Assyrian and more especially by Phœnician influences. The world knows what, in the hands of a composite race, endowed with the highest artistic faculties that have ever been found among men, these various traditions have called forth in Hellas. After a certain time of incubation, a style was produced bearing but a distant relation to that of preceding civilizations, and the creation of an ideal which has retained its superiority in high plastic work.

Under the influence of these arts, ornamentation likewise underwent a remarkable change. Greek ornament, less hieratic than the Egyptian, less restricted to the narrow use of the symbol, less spiritualistic and more living, possesses greater liberty, pliancy and grace, which were never abused, but always kept within bounds by the good taste of the Greeks.

Always pure, noble and elevated, ingenious and varied, but never luxuriant or excessive, Greek ornament bore the stamp of those superior qualities which raised architecture, sculpture, and the other plastic arts to such an elevation, but at the same time, and as a natural consequence of the development of the other forms of art, a secondary rank was assigned to ornament, almost always subordinated to the interest of the figures of men or animals, which wind round the vases, and people the metopes and friezes.

If we seek now, from the point of view announced in the commencement of this study, the principal character in Greek ornament, we shall find it to be clearly *conventional* (when it is not purely ideal) and though inspired by the general forms found in nature, free from a servile imitation of details.

A rapid enumeration of its favourite motives will enable us to recognize this ruling character of Greek ornament. Thus the graceful *palmette* of which the antifixæ are formed, which play so important a part on the friezes of the temples, as well as on the bowls and necks of vases, is taken from the pods of the carob tree, variously united and twisted into branches, plumes, etc.; but the variation from nature is so great that it may be considered as a real creation, almost as much so as the meanders, cable mouldings, etc. Some other *palmettes*, taken from different plants, such as the aloe and the convolvulus, designs composed with leaves of water plants, ivy, laurel, or vine complete the ordinary flora of Greek ornament, the most celebrated type of which is that *acanthus leaf* which decorates the Corinthian capital,

Fragment of a Stela, from Asia Minor, with *palmette* and acanthus leaves.
(Taken from the " *Expédition scientifique en Morée,*" by Blouet. 3 volumes, folio ; Paris, Firmin Didot.)

concerning which Vasari has handed down to us the charming fable. " That acanthus stem, oh Callimachus, the sculptor! that acanthus stem," cries Ziegler, " which you found richly growing in a place of sepulture, and with which you decorated the capital, the glory of the Corinthian name, that irrepressible acanthus has passed through twenty-two centuries, without losing one of its leaves, and has covered with its branches the whole monumental world."

Symmetry and regularity are the general principles of Greek decoration ; everything was made to yield to these rules :—" Even the white crests of the waves of the sea," says M. Jacquemart, in speaking of the Vitruvian scrolls, " so often frayed by the winds, seemingly essentially variable and capricious, are brought under the yoke of ornamental regularity; painters have transformed them into the elegant Vitruvian scrolls which the ancients had the sense to place always at the base of goblets, whilst among us, through ignorance of their signification, they are frequently placed where they are perfectly meaningless." (Examples of these may be seen in Plate V. Nos. 11, 12, 13 and 14, and in Plate VI. No. 19.)

The other principal elements of Greek ornament, a part of which is especially suited to architecture, are :

Meanders or *Frets*, interlacings of straight lines broken and cut at right angles, many examples of which may be seen in Plates V. and VI., and the use of which was so frequent in Hellenic art that they are frequently called *Greek frets*.

Cable Mouldings, combinations of curved lines, penetrating regularly into each other (Plate VI. Nos. 16, 25, 26, 27, 29). They are sometimes simple and sometimes double. (Nos. 16 and 25.)

Trellised Mouldings or plaits, an imitation of a plait of hair.

Chaplets or *Astragals* are composed of a number of round and oval bodies seemingly strung together, and which probably represent the necklaces worn by women.

Ogees, showing flowers and leaves of water plants (See Plate V. Nos. 13, 14, 15, and Plate VI. No. 3).

Channellings, short flutings, the ground of which is filled with pointed leaves (See Plate VI. No. 17).

Greek Trellised Mouldings.   Greco-Roman Frieze.   (Acanthus Leaves, Egg-mouldings and Chaplets of Pearls.)
(Taken from the " *Description de l'Asie Mineure*," by Ch. Texier ; Paris, Firmin Didot.)

Egg-mouldings, ornaments cut in the shape of an egg, which frequently take the form of such fruit as the chestnut, the shell being left open.

Bucranes, ornaments designed from the ox's skull. Leathern bands or thongs, horns decorated with flowers or jewels, or else garlands and wreaths of flowers nearly always accompany them. These bands

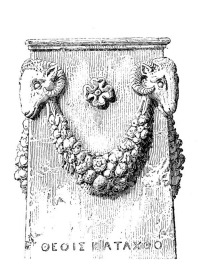

Bucranes, Egg-mouldings and Astragals.
(Subject taken from the " *Description de l'Asie Mineure*," by Ch. Texier.)

and adornments remained fastened to the horns of a victim, and, after the sacrifice, were suspended with his head from the walls of temples, tombs or altars. The artificial reminder of these offerings becomes a chief feature of noble decoration on the friezes of temples, and like all that the Greeks touched, turned in their hands into a fresh source of beauty.

Modern art has not abandoned these charming and fertile inventions, some of which are common to

Greek and other arts (such, for instance, as the *meander*, which is to be found everywhere, and the taste for which seems innate in man), whilst others belong more especially to Hellenic art. Without speaking of architecture, the decorative arts still derive most useful instruction from these productions of ancient Greece.

The colouring in Greek ornament, as well as the form, is always *conventional*. It was used very frequently, for the Greeks applied polychromatic decoration to numerous branches of art.

Architecture may be mentioned as the first of these. It is now beyond question that this art was frequently polychromatic. The skilful restorations by our artists, and especially by the holders of our art scholarships at Rome, have assisted largely in demonstrating this fact, which receives frequent confirmation in the fresh researches and discoveries of scholars and artists. Plate VI. presents some interesting examples of architectural colouring.

Mosaic, the very nature of which is based on the employment of materials of various colours, is likewise essentially polychromatic.

Incrustation of metals also derives its principal effect from the opposition and blending of tints, and was much admired by the Greeks.

And lastly, colour is the principal ornament of *Keramics*, the importance of which has induced us to give up to it an entire plate of the two that we were able to devote to pure Greek ornament.

This manufacture spread over the rest of Greece and even Italy, from Corinth, the city of potters; and indeed many of the vases found in Apulia and Etruria were of Greek fabrication.

Some of these vases were already in existence in the time of Homer. In the most ancient known, the style resembles the Egyptian, and these would date from ten or twelve centuries before the Christian era; the designs are usually black on a light ground, and the details of the models seem to have been taken from embroideries. Nos. 1, 7, 8, 9, 10 and 26 of Plate V. belong to this style and period. The employment of black ground is of a later date; it was in use at the time when Greek art was at its highest development. Nos. 17, 18, 19 and 20 of the same plate belong to this manner; they come from Apulia, and show by their variety and freedom of treatment all the resources of the style.

Etruscan (Plate VII.).—Before examining what Greek art became on an Italian soil, we mus speak of an art contemporary with that of the Greeks, and which was, in some degree, merged into it to form the Greco-Roman style.

The art of the Etruscans, who inhabited the centre of Italy, dated from the most remote antiquity.

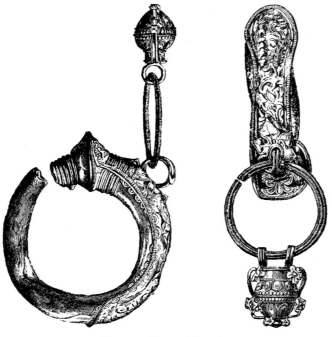

Etruscan Funeral Jewels.
(Taken from "*Etrurie et les Etrusques*," by M. Noël Des Vergers.[1])

Their race is supposed to have been formed from indigenous as well as from Pelasgic and Phœnician elements, and, in this mingling Winkelmann discerns the hardy race from whom the Tuscans have sprung. They became the artists of the Romans, and built their ancient edifices.

Independently of their keramics, always celebrated, but now usually considered as belonging to the Egyptian or Greek style, either through imitation or importation, the Etruscans had made great advances in goldsmith's work, and it is to this national product that Plate VII. has been devoted.

The skill of the Etruscan goldsmiths was celebrated in ancient times. Their jewels in embossed or chased gold were appreciated and much sought after, even at Athens. They knew and practised every resource of this art and carried it to perfection; under their skilful hand everything was made to lend its assistance: flowers, fruits, real or fantastic animals, human, heroic, or deified figures, alternating with vases of all forms, with acorns, discs, cornucopiæ, intermixed with rose work, crescents, flattened or lentil-shaped balls, with chains of every sort of work and of all sizes, intermingled with emeralds, to

---

[1] Those of our readers who wish to know more of the Etruscan style may advantageously consult this very interesting work.

which medicinal virtues were attributed, and the peculiar green of which harmonizes so well with the yellow of gold, pearls, glass-paste, enamels, cameos, intaglios : a union effected with such good taste in so great a variety, that many of these jewels are still considered masterpieces of their kind.

They consist of diadems and crowns, hair-pins, ear-drops, necklaces, fibulæ, bracelets, rings, objects of worship, and funeral jewels.

Scarabæi are frequently introduced in necklaces, bracelets and rings ; they usually unite the work of the intaglio and the cameo ; their under surface, flat and hollowed out, contains either hieroglyphics or various figures. The upper part, on the contrary, always convex, is sculptured in relief and represents in a more or less complete manner the Egyptian scarabæus, from the use of which not merely on jewels but also on clothing, necklaces, utensils and sword hilts we may probably infer, if not a direct worship as amongst the Egyptians, at all events some superstitious ideas.

The Intaglios or deepening, for which the Greeks at the finest periods of their art had a marked predilection, and of which the Etruscans also made great use, were usually transparent and of a single colour. Amongst precious stones, properly so called, the amethyst, hyacinth, and sometimes the opaque emerald were especially chosen ; from the others the cornelian, the chalcedony, and more rarely the jasper and lapis-lazuli.

Under the Roman dominion and the ever-increasing invasion of Greek art, the productions of Etruria lose their peculiar character, and the indigenous works yield completely to the foreign influence.

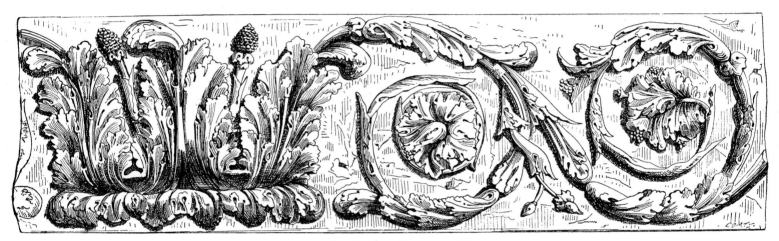

Acanthus Leaf. (Roman scroll.)

We turn then naturally to the development of Greco-Roman art, which terminates the cycle of ancient art properly so called.

Greco-Roman. (Plates VIII., IX.)—The ancient Romans possessed nothing of their own worthy the name of art. After the first period of that art which they were indebted for to their Etruscan builders, a period characterized especially in Architecture by the use of the vault and arcades, and the modifications it entailed in the use of ornament, we have just seen that the workmen of Etruria, losing their primitive originality by contact with the Greek colonies, assumed by degrees all the traditions of the latter. There was then no longer any art in Italy but the Greek, after the arrival of the objects of art brought by Marcellus from Syracuse, by Mummius from Corinth, and by all the Roman generals after them. Conquered Greece had become through her arts in her turn the conqueror. Those master-pieces which rendered Rome an enormous museum determined the direction of Roman taste.

The paintings of Pompeii and Herculaneum are, according to our most learned archæologists and artists, of the same kind as the paintings that adorned the houses in Athens. (See Hittorff, " *L'Architecture polychrome chez les Grecs,*" chapter IX. entitled " *Lettres d'un Antiquaire à un Artiste,*" by Letronne.)

" In decorative painting applied to dwelling-houses, the competent archæologist accepts as a fact that the Romans took everything from the Hellenes, both in taste and the means of satisfying it; that the Greek artists carried on their art at Rome and in all Italy as they had practised it in their own country; in short, that the Romans accepted their inheritance, and that, as a consequence, the decoration of the ancient Roman dwellings, and the houses of Pompeii and Herculaneum, the paintings in which are exclusively Greek in manner and execution, must give an exact idea of the similar decoration which adorned the houses of Greece, not only at a contemporaneous epoch, but also at an anterior time."

These paintings are not all of the same value. A certain number appear to have been executed by inferior artists; but the beauty of some makes us think that they were copies and repetitions of Greek works of great celebrity.

Besides decorative painting, we find at Pompeii, in some degree of perfection, another application of polychromatic colouring in mosaic.

But this latter branch of art underwent in the hands of the Romans, from the times of the Empire, some modifications which have been explained with great truth by M. Jeanron in his book entitled " *Origines et Progrès de l'Art*," in a passage which we think it better to quote, notwithstanding its length, because in this particular art it allows us to follow the history of the decay of Greek art in the last period of Roman civilization.

" The Romans," says this eminent critic, " who possessed a knowledge of mosaic in a rudimentary state, received it, like every other process in art, from the hands of the Greeks, in a more advanced state. Soon their love of luxury, their contempt of expense, caused it to spread widely among them and to arrive at real progress, as the monuments that have been discovered amply prove . . . The Romans were not long, however, in perverting the nature of what the Greeks had transmitted to them. The exquisite taste of the latter, their understanding of the distribution of ornament, their advanced imitative science, could not but have enabled them to realize charming conceptions in mosaic. But assuredly the good

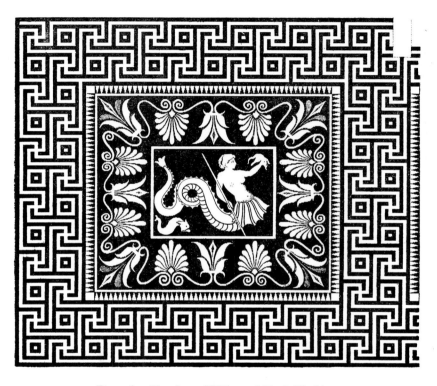

Pompeian Mosaic.   (White and black Marble.)

(Taken from the " *Expédition scientifique en Morée*," by Blouet.)

sense of the Greeks could never have brought mosaic into contention with the highest prerogatives of painting. The Greeks, it is supposed, had made the compartment of their paved floors represent ornaments, branches, scrolls, festoons, interlacings ; and passing onward from these capricious forms, somewhat of the nature of arabesques, to symbols and attributes more significant, they had adopted griffins, chimeras, tragic or comic masks, the signs of the zodiac, vine branches, birds pecking fruits and all the well-known motives of their ornamentation. It may even be admitted that the idea must frequently have occurred to them to set in the centre of the formal arrangements of some rich pavement a scene of the kind that they treated with so much grace and simplicity : nymphs asleep or giving water to some fantastic animal, dancers, actors, players on the flute or castanets. It is thus that the finest antique mosaics are arranged : the one that was found at Otricoli during the last century, and which is the finest ornament in the circular hall of the Pio-Clementino Museum ; that of Italica, and the famous Prænestine, which paved the splendid temple of Fortune at Præneste under Sylla.

" But, as is well known, when the Romans liked anything they carried it to an excess. Cæsar, before this time, by his own order was followed into the heart of Gaul by workers in marble ; and, all through his expeditions, the compartments of the *opus tesselatum et sectile* (varieties of mosaic) were laid hastily in his tent. And at a later time, Heliogabalus, thinking that, on the day when Rome, or rather his Prætorians, should be tired of him, he might have to dash his brains out upon the pavement of his courtyard, caused it to be inlaid with precious stones.

" But long before the time of Heliogabalus, the Romans, who loved mosaics and wished to have them everywhere, were no longer satisfied with adorning the floors of their courts and lower rooms with them ; they also decorated the walls, the arches and the ceilings. From what Pliny says we might even imagine that this last plan was more followed than the other, that the mosaics were thought too beautiful to be trampled under foot any longer, and that they wished to enjoy them as pictures."

Here M. Jeanron shows that pebbles, stones, natural or coloured marbles, paste and terra-cotta, shells and fragments of pots, being no longer able to contend with the colours of painting—especially during a time when painters, impelled by a mad love of brilliancy and richness, borrowed from red lead, purple, azure, gold and silver, their deceptive glitter and striking oppositions—mosaic demanded fresh resources in various precious stones, such as agate, jasper, cornelian, sardonyx, emerald, turquoise, lapis-lazuli, in short, from all the colours of enamels, to imitate every fancy of the painter with his seven or eight principal colours.

"This idea was false," continues M. Jeanron, "for had the worker in mosaic had more shades at his service, and the painter fewer colours, it would even then have been an unequal strife. But the centuries of political decay which witnessed the greatest triumphs of mosaic, well explain pretensions and triumphs. In the later times of the empire the requirements of luxury daily narrowed the domain of art, and the pursuit of a false brilliancy gave to artists a merely feverish activity. Painting had come to be nothing but an ambitious collection of colours, in which the

Mosaic.
(Taken from "*Herculanum et Pompéi*," by Roux and Barré; Paris, Firmin Didot.)

rawest tints were united to the poorest forms. Mosaic being more costly, more glittering to the eye and smoother to the touch, could not but dethrone its rival; thus this deplorable revolution was actuated by no idea at all approaching to a higher character. Mosaic, restricted by its very nature, submitted to the most ungrateful handiwork, unable to carry out its idea immediately, but obliged to go through the wearisome and lengthy process of calking and cutting, soon forgot all that painting had succeeded in teaching it and became a mere manufacture. The workers

Greco-Roman Frieze.

in mosaic soon left off drawing for themselves the subjects they intended to execute with their enamels; they passed about from one to another, as a stock-in-trade, the cartoons and pounced drawings that were needed. Now, when it is remembered that, notwithstanding the deplorable degeneracy of its only artistic parts, mosaic had none the less taken from painting its finest and noblest undertakings, it will be clearly seen how rapid the decay must have been in all the arts of design."

At last, with the reign of the Syrian princes, and the invasion of Eastern religions, there came an influx of magic and sensualism absorbing everything before them, and science and observation vanished under a love of the supernatural and unbridled luxury. Cameos became amulets, medals talismans, and under these circumstances, the clear, measured art of the Greeks, on a foreign soil and with the ideas of another race, was doomed to completely disappear. The last and faintest expression of this art is to be found in the paintings in the catacombs of Rome, the symbolic ornamentation of which is an hieroglyphic language framed to meet new wants.

APPENDIX ON CHROMATICS.

WE do not propose to treat questions of chromatics by figures merely, as so many ingenious observers, unable to work with the colour itself, have been obliged to do. We are happily able to produce numerous coloured examples which, notwithstanding their occasionally unfavourable juxtaposition, will speak to the eye of the observer with greater force, and we believe with more success than any physiological commentary.

However, the paintings that we have taken from Pompeii, show compositions of such value, both from the simple nature of the means employed and the result obtained, that we think it well to introduce the theory in order to show what a perfect knowledge the ancients possessed of the resources of colour, and of its mutual relations. In the first place we must remark that in the painted wall of the *Casa delle suonatrici* (Plate VIII.) the effect sought is the throwing into relief a construction made *ad hoc*, on a ground which is rendered aërial; and that this double effect is obtained by plain colours without shading, by their mere chromatic value. As we shall see presently, nothing can better demonstrate the justness and depth of the technical knowledge of the Greeks in decoration. The blue ground in imitation of the sky is everywhere of the same intensity; the effect of gradation, that is to say of the upper part predominating and the lower appearing more distant and lighter, which produces the aërial look, is the result of practised reasoning, in perfect harmony with the statements of modern physics on advancing and retreating colours.

We borrow from the remarkable book of Dr. Ernest Brücke,[1] a part of his chapter on this theory of advancing and retreating colours, which will be useful through the whole course of this work.

" The eye works like a camera-obscura. All the light emitted by a distinctly visible point which penetrates into this organ unites again in a single point on the retina.

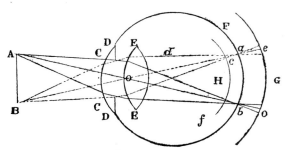

The Eye and the projection of Rays.

" A B, object; C C, transparent cornea; D D, iris and pupil; E E, crystalline lens; O, optical centre of the crystalline lens; C A C and C B E, luminous divergent cones emitted by A and B, falling on the eye; C B C and C A E, luminous cones rendered convergent by the successive refractions in the aqueous humour, the crystalline lens and the vitreous humour; *a b*, reversed image of the object.

" It may be seen that according as the retina is in F, H or G, the image received will be clear or indistinct. There is thus formed a reversed image of the object.

" In the same way as the arrangement of the camera-obscura has to be changed according to the greater or less distance of objects, if the clearness of the image is to be preserved, so the eye requires a special adaptation for each distance. We produce this effect by the contraction of a muscle, which provokes certain modifications in the internal arrangement of the eye. We cannot here enter more into details on this question. The reader will find it treated of in any work on physiology. We have but an imperfect knowledge of this method of adaptation.

" When all the means which we usually employ to appreciate the distance of an object fails us, when we know nothing of its true size, when neither the surrounding objects, nor the aërial perspective give us any assistance, we experience a vague sensation which tells us whether the object be near or distant.

" This sentiment is connected with the nature of advancing and retreating colours, in the following way: rays of short vibration (they will be represented presently) are more strongly refracted than those of long duration when they pass obliquely from one medium to another. These rays then converge in our eye sooner than those of long vibrations, emitted by the same luminous point.

" It results from this, that two *luminous points* unequally distant from the eye, one of which is red, the other blue, may emit rays which will unite by convergence at the same distance from the crystalline lens, supposing, however, that the red point is the more distant.

Convergence at the same distance from the Crystalline Lens of two luminous Points unequally distant from the Eye.

---

[1] " *Die Physiologie der Farben für die Zwecke der Kunstgewerbe,*" by Dr. Ernest Brücke, Professor of Physiology at the University of Vienna. " *Des Couleurs au point de vue physique, physiologique, artistique et industriel,*" par le Dr. Ernest Brücke. Traduit par J. Schützenberger ; Paris, J. B. Baillière, 1866.

" Let R be the red point, B the blue point a little nearer ; both form their image at an equal distance from the crystalline lens, and, if this distance coincide with that of the retina, we shall see the two coloured points with the same clearness, by one and the same arrangement. The peculiar state of the eye is now no longer capable of telling us that the two points R and B are not at equal distances from it. We will now take the point D, which we will suppose blue. To receive a clear image on the retina of this point, the eye has to undergo a slight modification, and be accommodated to a greater distance. If the blue point B seems to us as distant as the red point R, it is clear that the blue point D will appear more distant.

" When looking from a certain distance at coloured windows, formed by red and blue squares, surrounded by a black grating, it seems as if the red were more prominent than the blue, and were actually standing out ; the black spaces formed by the grating give the effect of oblique planes leading to the background of blue glass. The inverse result is never seen.

" The advancing colours are, red, orange and yellow. The retreating colours belong to the various categories of blue ; blue and violet are intermediate ; green is advancing in relation to blue, and especially to ultramarine ; it is retreating in comparison with red, orange and yellow.

" . . . . . . If we bring forward the advancing colour, and place in the background the retreating colour, we increase the effect of the illusion ; in the contrary case, we diminish it . . . .

" Certain designs can awaken in us impressions as of their being in relief, though vague, and as if seen dimly in a dream ; the charm exercised by these designs is produced precisely by this effect. It may easily be seen that the retreating or advancing properties of a colour must have a marked influence on the production of such phenomena, and that an exact knowledge of these characters is well calculated to render important services in the composition of colours."

We will not insist any longer on this subject, it is easy to make an application of this complete theory in the example given : the brilliant red, the orange, and yellow, and then the retreating blue colour calculated to give a greater distance ; green is the intermediate part, and, lastly, in the upper part and approaching the blue ground, the absence of orange and the red softening down into pink, and losing its advancing intensity. What completes the value of this mural painting, is that theory further demonstrates that an artificial light of wax or oil, far from weakening this effect, only renders it the more powerful. It is, indeed, the completion of the theory on this subject, that the yellow of artificial lights, by adding to the intensity of the red, orange and yellow, increases their brilliancy, whilst the yellow produces a contrary effect on the blue, which, as it repels it, becomes only the more retreating.

Mosaic.

ASIATIC ART.

UNDER this title of Asiatic art, as the second of the two fertile sources from which modern art has derived its models, we include all the decorative arts of what is usually called the East, as well as of the extreme East. This arrangement comprises in the same class the productions of very different periods, the most ancient of which may even surpass in antiquity the work of the Egyptians themselves, whilst the most recent are almost contemporary with ourselves. Considered however in its general features this vast subject is less complicated than would appear at first sight.

The traditional immobility of the East, where the processes of fabrication and the practices of art are transmitted faithfully from generation to generation, frequently renders it extremely difficult to assign a precise date to any one production. And, indeed, unless it be as a matter of curiosity, or as affecting the real value of the object, there attaches usually but little interest to such an investigation, at least with regard to the general characters of the ornamentation which modern decorators have taken with more or less sincerity from ancient models, frequently producing the most complete illusion.

Freed in this way from the necessity of a minute chronological examination, our short treatise may confine itself to broad divisions describing the primary and original styles which predominate over the lesser divisions and personal modifications.

From our special point of view, without entering into the examination of very interesting ethnographical questions, beyond the scope of our book as well as of our ability, we recognize three principal groups or families : the Chinese family, the Indian family, and the Arabian family. (See Anquetil Duperron and Champollion Figeac, "*Histoire de la Perse.*")

The group comprising China and Japan, will be treated first and alone, as befits its genius and history.

Then returning to the East, properly so called, we will examine separately the two great Indian and Arabian traditions, going over their distinctive characteristics, and also their points of meeting. The principal point of union in these is to be found in Persian art, which came originally from India, but was much modified by the Mahomedan style on the triumph of Islam and the Arab conquest.

CHINESE AND JAPANESE.

Plates X. to XV.

Chinese.

TURNING to the Chinese, a nation of the highest antiquity, we find that, during its long existence, this people, or rather this world, seems to have neither given nor received anything from other civilizations from time immemorial; it has always sufficed for itself, and in this immobility and isolation, which form its originality, it has created a style for itself, without any relation to the productions of other nations, if, however, we except certain geometric combinations which instinct has given to every known race.

The extreme fancifulness of their ornamental compositions, and the want of order and method usually seen in them, may be understood if we consider that the Chinese have no architectural art in our sense of the word, no archetype of idealization, giving rise to ornaments in which even the most insignificant designs are invested with a character of grandeur, as is amply exemplified in Egyptian ornamentation. "This absence of architecture," says M. de Chavannes de la Giraudière, "is in the genius of the Chinese nation. This people seems bound to occupy itself exclusively with details, and this too in everything. The conception of a monumental building is above its comprehension."

We will complete this observation by saying that the light and graceful dwellings of the Chinese are all derived from the idea of the tent, the instability and size of which exclude the grander characters of architecture.[1] This circumstance has certainly contributed largely amongst the Chinese to leaving the arts of design in a simple and rudimentary state, and it likewise explains why we so rarely meet with simplicity and amplitude in their ornamentations.

Amongst the Chinese, moreover, variety constitutes the first element of beauty. In their ornamental screens, leaves following each other bear no resemblance; by the side of a compartment representing a landscape there will be another of brilliant colours, and covered with metallic arabesques. They take the greatest pains to avoid the straight line and right angle, or, to disguise them when they do make use of them, they torture the imagination, or rather give free play to their disordered imagination, in their curiously shaped furniture, the real intention of which they endeavour to conceal by a pretence of a totally different destination.

To such conceptions, so different from our own, and so completely destitute of the conditions of true grandeur that any change of proportion is at once fatal to the design, and in which, except for a screen or a blind, the interest it may excite is with difficulty maintained, we must add that the Chinese pay no attention to the laws of perspective, and do not understand the play of shadows or of chiaroscuro.

And yet, notwithstanding so many conditions of fundamental inferiority, their ornament is

---

[1] Pagodas and triumphal arches, excessively numerous in China, are the only exceptions to this rule. The pagodas, nearly all constructed on the same model, only differ from each other in height, richness of ornament and beauty of materials. They alone are of a really monumental character. ("*Les Chinois*," by H. de Chavannes de la Giraudière.) Chinese palaces, notwithstanding the dimensions and rich decorations of some of them, have scarcely any other character.

treated with so much imagination, their colouring is so rich, and they make such a varied and charming use of it, that in certain particular applications, such as keramics, incrustations, and woven materials, their productions are models of harmony and effect, which have remained in many points superior to the works of other nations.

Their defects are the source of good qualities which correspond to them, and one effect of their capricious mobility is that they are full of resources, making an ornament out of everything, from the cloud and the wave, the shell and the rock, from the animated world of reality as well as that of fancy, from flowers in every variety and wrought woods, the flaming thunderbolt and the sparkling insect, from vases of every shape and objects of every form, crystals, scrolls, writing, &c.

To these ornamental resources, at once so rich and so varied, may be added a certain number of time-honoured figures, having in general a symbolical signification. Amongst these may be mentioned the dragons, monsters armed with powerful claws and having a frightful head with

formidable-looking teeth, so many varieties of which are to be met with in Chinese compositions: dragons with scales, winged, horned, without horns, rolling over themselves before taking their flight into higher regions. Another of these symbols is the dog of Fo, whose claws, sharp teeth and curly mane constitute a lion, modified by fancy; also the sacred horse; the Fong-Hoang, a singular bird, with its head adorned with caruncles, a silky neck, and a tail between that of an argus and a peacock, whose presence is of happy augury; then the white stag, the axis, the crane, the mandarin duck, all figures which have their own proper interpretation in Chinese decoration.

It is a singular circumstance that this art, which appears so capricious and chimerical in its conceptions, is characterized in its execution by such an immutability of proceeding and faithfulness of transmission in the representation of things, that it frequently requires the lapse of hundreds of years before even the slightest modification can be perceived.

This phenomenon may be merely the effect of the essentially imitative and traditional instinct of this isolated civilization, so advanced in some points, so barbarous in others, but always consistent to itself. Perhaps, also, this fidelity in the observance of the same proceeding in the employment of forms and colours comes from some mysterious rules, some sort of ritual, perpetuated through so many ages.

This last explanation may find its confirmation in a sort of symbol of forms and fundamental colours, an analysis of which we borrow from the learned work of M. Jacquemart, "*Les Merveilles de la Céramique.*"

"The colours are fixed at five in the "Memorial of Rites," 2205 years B. C. They are to be found in the Tcheou-li (Rites dating from the twelfth to the eighth century before the Christian era).

"The work of embroiderers in colours consists in combining these five colours.

"The side on the east is blue. The side on the south is red. The side on the west is white. The side on the north is black. The side towards the sky is blackish blue. The side of the earth is yellow. The blue combines with the white. The red combines with the black. The blackish blue combines with the yellow.

"The earth is represented by the yellow colour; its special figure is the square. The sky varies according to the seasons.

"Fire is represented by the figure of a circle. Water is represented by the figure of a dragon. Mountains are represented by a deer.

"Birds, quadrupeds, reptiles are represented according to nature."

The imperial livery has changed according to the dynasties; it has been white, then green, it is now yellow for the Tai-Tsing dynasty, still reigning in China.

If we now examine Chinese art relatively to the principal categories placed at the head of this historical sketch, we find in it a mixture of the *ideal* and *imitative* elements; but the latter used in a *conventional* manner.

The colouring is also conventional, not in the least subject to any imitation of natural colours, and in this respect the chromatics of the Chinese (which possibly obey laws of another kind) possess complete liberty.

The applications of ornament in Chinese art are most varied.

All movable light objects, such as blinds, screens, boxes, fans, &c., are especially adapted for Chinese decoration.

The manufacture of woven fabrics also finds in it many very effective subjects.

The lineal element of the *meanders* is employed with such marked superiority in the incrusted bronzes and the *cloisonné* enamels as would alone suffice to raise the art of the Chinese to a high rank, even if their keramics did not place them first in that branch of art.

In the decorations of the Kaolinic pottery, the genius of the Chinese has soared to its greatest height. They excel in throwing in cartouches of every shape, being sometimes of unequal dimensions, at others regular, round, oval, polygonal, imitating the outline of a fruit or leaf, or very frequently of a fan,

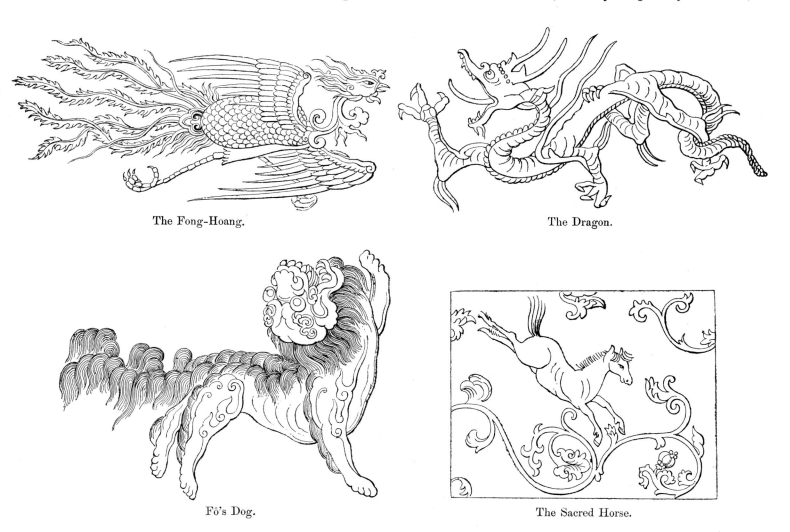

The Fong-Hoang.

The Dragon.

Fô's Dog.

The Sacred Horse.

and they dispose them as if by chance on grounds of geometrical construction. They people these enclosed spaces with landscapes, containing manufacturing buildings, mountains, rocks, groups of flowers, and fantastic or real animals. This art is considered to have reached its greatest height between 1465 and 1487, a period when the most curious combinations were to be seen.

In our days China is in a state of decay, the causes of which are complex, the principal being, certainly, the excessive division of labour, as it is now practised. Father d'Entrecolles tells us that in one manufactory, "the occupation of one man is merely to form the first coloured circle near the edge of the porcelain; another sketches flowers which a third paints; one is for water and mountains, another for birds, another for animals, and so on."

With such methods, all individuality disappears. Thus, the Chinese themselves attach a far higher value to the old works, especially in bronzes, enamels, and vases, than to the new, which are little more than imitations.

Japanese.—Japanese art is an offspring from the Chinese, but is distinguished by a greater individuality, as they seem to have escaped the danger of the excessive division of artistic labour as it is practised in modern China. The Japanese have developed the study of nature, especially in birds, with more truthfulness and power of observation than their ancestors or rivals, which renders their *imitative* style less conventional. However, it must be confessed that if their delicate productions have added fresh charms to the old Chinese keramics, they frequently lose much of the vigour of the finest periods. Decoration sometimes requires a voluntary roughness, and a soberness in the use of means, of which they have not always felt the excellence. To the Chinese colours the Japanese have added their own, and it is this which serves principally to distinguish the productions of the two countries. The art of the Japanese is at present tending towards fresh developments; their ornamentation, better regulated than it was, is in the hands of skilful draughtsmen, who observe nature, know how to round off their forms, and understand the laws of perspective. One of the principal causes of the general progress is to be found in the fact of the incredible profusion with which models of all sorts, conceived by really good artists, and carved in wood, are distributed among the public. There lies an element of progress from a certain point of view, but which can perhaps scarcely be continued without some detriment to the originality, until now so distinct, of Chinese and Japanese productions.

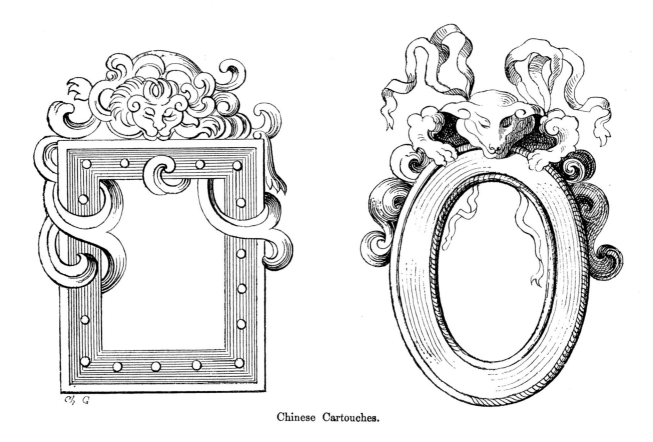

Chinese Cartouches.

APPENDIX ON CHROMATICS.

WE have given an extract from the " Memorial of Chinese Rites," which would possess merely an archæological interest if it were not for the fact that under this symbolism the soundest laws of chromatics are concealed.

The symbolism of colours, enunciated by the " Chinese Rites," is in reality nothing but a statement of the only primitive colours recognized by painters, which Ziegler (in his " *Histoire de la Céramique*") has brought out clearly from the spectral combinations, setting aside the blendings of the latter as misleading.

These primitive colours are:—1st, yellow; 2nd, red; 3rd, blue, *undecomposable;* 4th, black, which, unless absolutely negative, that is to say, arising from the absence of light, is acknowledged to be the maximum of intensity in every primitive colour (for there are blacks of all sorts), and which consequently becomes the most powerful generating principle; 5th, white, undecomposed light, which is the maximum of brilliancy in every colour.

We may learn much by studying the different gradations of colours as these masters in harmony have understood them, as following each other in systematic order. This study must be accompanied by observation of the means employed, either for isolating the colours or for uniting them, means applied some-times in an absolute manner and sometimes according to the need and nature of the colouring, by using simultaneously every method of isolation and of uniting of colour at the same time.

In the *cloisonné* enamels, Plates XI. and XII., the gilded outline is a medium both of separa-tion and of union.

In Plate XIII. and the lower part of Plate XIV. the white outline is a medium of isolation (the most powerful for this purpose) and is quite indispensable; it is only the intense blue of the one and the dark green of the other which can do without it.

In the upper part of Plate XIV. the outlines are reddish brown or black, sometimes weak or entirely wanting; this is just what was required for procuring lightness of ground with proportioned intensities, without injuring the delicacy of the objects represented. It may be seen that this ap-propriation of outlines deserves special study; for supposing them altered or suppressed, the subjects would be entirely spoiled, and the combination of the colours employed rendered quite impossible. The application of the same principle may be seen in the running patterns forming Plate XV., which closes this series.

INDIAN—ARABIAN AND MOORISH—PERSIAN.

PLATES XVI. TO XXX.

Indian.

ALTHOUGH less isolated than the Chinese, and coming more into contact with the rest of the world, Indian civilization, notwithstanding its extreme antiquity, has not experienced those changes which mark the history of so many other nations.

The social and religious organizations, priests, temples, castes, sacred books, poetry, manners, doctrines and superstitions still remain much as they were amongst the Hindoos, whom even the conquest of their country has been unable to deprive of their own distinctive character and institutions.

Art must naturally have shared to a great degree in this characteristic immobility, and notwith-standing some unimportant modifications, which a glance at Arabian and Persian art will enable us better to understand, the substance of Indian decoration may still be defined by certain salient features which have undergone no fundamental alteration.

The most striking of these characteristics are perhaps the *continuity* and *plenitude* of decoration which usually entirely fills up the surface to be decorated with a profusion of ornaments either exactly alike or of similar nature; the design being in general a simple repetition of the same subject. The colour of the ground, always warm and harmonious, occasionally light though more frequently dark, serves to unite the designs, besides being the principal agent in the general effect. This method of distribution, applied with an admirable feeling for colour, procures in Indian decoration a richness and calm which give an indefinable sensation of repose, and the only fault in which would be monotony, if this powerful unity could leave room for a desire or a need for greater variety.

The designs themselves are nearly all taken from the floral world treated in a conventional manner, in which, however, although the generalized type predominates over the varieties of the species, the imitation bears a closer resemblance to nature than in most of the styles we have studied until now. Without any servile imitation, the model is generally easily recognized, and although the floral ornament is sometimes seen under the pure, hard form of the Egyptian style, it is more frequently treated with a pliancy of execution and picturesqueness which makes it bear a closer resemblance to the modern style.[1]

Indian palm.

This execution however never attains to rounding off of forms, a process in general foreign to the decoration of surfaces amongst the Orientals, it is usually confined to silhouette drawings in which the outline is usually shown off by a darker tint on light grounds, and by a lighter colour on dark grounds.

We believe that we are not mistaken in giving these characteristics as typical of the primary and original form of Indian decoration, a form still predominant, notwithstanding the more frequent intervention of the constructive element, borrowed from the Arabs, and modified by the Persians, whose style, as we shall see presently, may be considered as the point of meeting and of union of the two great Arabian and Indian streams.

In recapitulating the points which unite these three arts we shall have to add a few words on the colouring of Indian ornament.

Arabian.—After the Indian style we come to that of the Arabs, which would appear to be posterior to the Indian, according to the general rule which causes the human mind to proceed from the simple to the complex.

Endowed with great genius, but forced to set aside any direct contact with nature from the prescription of the Koran, "Thou shalt make no images," the Arabs have substituted for the almost exclusively floral decoration of the Indians, the *constructed* ornament, the framing of which was an amusement to their geometrical minds, and the principal of which is that *Star of Solomon*, so much varied and enriched with secondary motives.

The continuity of the ornament entirely filling the surface is to be seen here as amongst the Indians, and in both styles nothing can be taken away without occasioning an unseemly void; the means employed, however, are different, and, whilst the mere repetition of subjects frequently suffices in

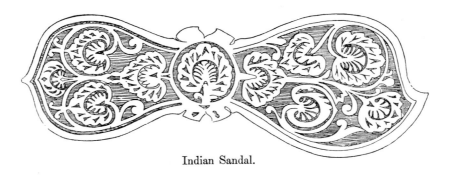

Indian Sandal.

Indian decoration, the Arabian ornament on the contrary is built up and bound together in all its parts; everything is connected, and in rose-work, for example, from the circumference to the centre all the interlacings take a common root in the ornament itself.

This imaginative construction is frequently double, that is to say, formed by two complete systems

---

[1] The Indian palm comes, more than any other element of floral decoration employed by the Indians, into the conventional style, as may be seen by the above figure. It is of very frequent recurrence in modern decoration, whether as an ornament symmetrically repeated in the borders, or as a sort of cartouche thrown into the midst of a floral design. It appears to belong to the Indo-Arabian style.

which follow each other to an end without confusion, but in which the meetings and overlappings produce incidental figures, intersections, and alternations relieved by colour from the ground, amidst the interlacings of foliage.

Notwithstanding this learned complication, Arabian decoration remains clear and distinct, thanks to the purity and fineness of the lines, and the general rule excluding all superfluity; and thanks, also, to the principle observed in the construction of the roses, which consists in reserving the wider

Star of Solomon.

Ornaments of Arabian construction.

(Designs taken from the "*Architecture arabe,*" by P. Coste. Paris, Firmin Didot.)

expansions for the extremities of the circumference, leaving to the radiating centre from which they diverge the fine work which throws out boldly, and fixes the eye on the key to the whole composition, as the central point of the circle.

We must add that the Arabians appear to have been the inventors of the ingenious design producing a double effect, the silhouette of which has two exteriors, tracing with a single line two opposite figures, as may be seen in No. 14 of Plate XVI. of Indian manufacture, though in the Arabian or Persian style, and also in Nos. 7 and 11 of Plate XXI. (Persian manufacture).

Arabian Rose-work.

But with a style thus conceived, what became of the floral element so valuable in decorative art?

In the primitive Arabian style, unmixed with Persian, the flower properly so called is not to be found, but in its place come other forms resembling it, and appearing directly inspired by nature. This sort of subject, half-way between imaginary conceptions and the representation of flowers properly so called, does not merely come in to terminate scrolls, as amongst the Greeks; they form an integral part of the decoration, and (as Owen Jones justly remarks in his "Grammar of Ornament"), they do not break the lineal net-work, they continue by constantly enlarging it.

Thus conceived and employed, the ornamental forms of the Arabs, in the original state and without Persian intermixture, being still more conventional than those of the Greeks, are of purely decorative conception, and are beyond and above nature.

To complete this rapid sketch of Arab ornament, we must add that it is completely free from a symbolism which was forbidden by their law. The Arabs consequently replaced symbolical writing by the use of real writing. Nothing is more common than to find running inscriptions in Cufic characters or running hand, forming a part of the decoration and producing the happiest effect; sometimes, indeed, they are introduced with such profusion that there is in existence one monument faced with glazed bricks in which the whole Koran runs through the arabesques.

Such are the principal features of this severe yet beautiful art, so strongly impressed with the Arabian genius that the term *Arabesque* still applies to the whole style of ornament which other nations have appropriated whilst recognizing its origin.

When speaking of Persian and Byzantine art we shall have occasion to say a few words on the contact of Arabian art with the Asiatic, and also with Greek and Greco-Roman art. Asia Minor, so frequently traversed by the conquerors of Persia, India, Egypt, and Syria, would offer many models well fitted to inspire them. But whatever may have been the effect of this contact, and without entering into the question of what the Arabs received and what they imparted, we believe that we see in their decorative system an original creation which belongs to themselves alone, and which furnished the primitive types before those fusions and meetings which may have modified it and given it intermediate styles.

Moorish.—Before altogether leaving Arabian art, we must speak of what it became in the hands of the Spanish Moors. It is merely a continuation of our subject; for the Moorish style, with a

Arabian Feather.

few distinguishing peculiarities of its own, belongs to the Arabian family. The mode of construction, the forms of ornament (especially the elegant *Arabian feather*), and the frequent use of inscriptions, are so many points in common between the Moorish *genre* and the pure Arabian style, which is seen to most advantage in the buildings of Cairo.

As a peculiar characteristic, we may mention in Moorish decoration, the more frequent use of a third ground placed over the two others and serving as a frame-work and link between them. It is slightly projecting, and is a real element of construction, sufficing without further change, to produce the open-work of which the Moors make such frequent use.

From a polychromatic point of view, the Moorish decoration is distinguished by a very generally adopted system, based on the principal employment of the three primary undecomposable colours, blue, red, and yellow represented by gold. In the facings and pavements, which assisted so well in developing the geometrical inventions of the Moors the colours are more numerous, and green plays often an important part.

It would be superfluous from our point of view and in the restricted limits of our work to dilate more fully on this Moorish art, the admirable monuments of which, constantly studied by the architect as well as by the decorator, have been so frequently described and analyzed.

Persian.—The recent labours of philology authorize us in supposing, that, in some unknown time of antiquity the whole of Iran belonged to the Indian family (Persia was the name of one of the provinces of Iran, and the temporary dominion of the Persians caused the name to be afterwards given to the whole) and that the origin of the civilization of Iran can be recognized only through that of India and its conquering dynasties. (See Champollion-Figeac, "*Histoire de la Perse.*") M. Batissier also remarks: "Persia has almost always formed a province of the vast empires founded by the different conquerors of Asia. Its history is thus intermingled with that of other nations."

What is true and historical with regard to the Arab, Seljookian Turk, Ottoman and Mongol invaders of Persia, is probably true also with regard to earlier invaders. But, beyond these historical conjectures on which we need give no opinion, a view of the productions of the two civilizations is a surer guide to us in ascribing an Indian origin to Persian ornament, which element became in time a firm tradition, and was afterwards blended with Arabian art.

From before the conquest which, next to the circumstance of the vicinity of the two races, brought about this latter period, the Persians were celebrated by their love of pomp and the perfection of their decorative arts. Thus, when after the defeat of the last of the Chosroes, the victorious Arabs took possession of Madayn, then the capital of Persia, these inhabitants of tents were much struck by the magnificent buildings, the luxury of the apartments and the ornaments of every kind which fell into their hands.[1] In the seventh century of our era, the Persians were living in splendour which seems to equal the most marvellous descriptions in the Râmâyana of ancient India (fifteenth century before the Christian era), accounts which are confirmed by Strabo, Arrianus and Megasthenes.

In the state in which we best know Persian art, at the period of its greatest splendour, the outlines are in general taken from the conceptions of Arabian architecture, modified both by Indian tradition and the peculiar genius of the Persian race, which tended towards a less compressed and austere style with more freedom and elegance than the Arabs possessed, and obtaining by its double derivation the elements of a greater variety.

Persian Inscription.

The floral element is employed in both its aspects, sometimes scattered through the decoration with apparent freedom, at others inserted in the lineal network, and usually placed at the intersection of lines; but, even in the latter case it is always treated in a manner which is a medium between the high Arab conventionality and the Indian quasi-naturalism.

We must likewise add, that, unlike the Arabs, who belonged to the sect of Omar, the Persian schismatics, drinkers of wine, belonging to the sect of Ali, and accustomed to attribute to flowers a symbolical language in the bouquets called Salams,[2] do not exclude the representation of flowers in their decoration, which is also animated by real and fantastic animals, and sometimes, though more rarely, by the human figure.

If, owing to these peculiarities, we usually succeed in distinguishing the productions of Arabian

---

[1] We read in Costa (*" Architecture Arabe "*) : " When after the battle of Kadesia (in the year 15 of the Hegira, 637 A.D.), the Arabs went towards Madayn, crowns, bracelets, golden necklaces . . . . fell into the hands of their commander, who divided the whole amongst his soldiers in conformity with the dispositions of the Koran. Amongst these objects was a carpet of sixty ells in length, of magnificent texture, representing a garden in which the flowers were precious stones woven into the fabric. The general-in-chief being doubtful as to the value of the booty, sent it to Omar, expressing a wish that it should be sold to the highest bidder, and the value distributed according to the law. Omar paid no attention to this request, and caused the rich carpet to be divided into pieces and distributed in equal portions. One portion, which fell to Ali, was sold by him for the sum of 20,000 drachmas." Comp. Gibbon, " Decline and Fall," chap. 51.

[2] The Persians are so fond of flowers that with them general rejoicings take place at the season for the flowering of tulips, a flower so frequently represented on their earthenware and enamelled bricks.

art (not, however, without some difficulty, and we may cite our Plates XXVII. and XXVIII. taken from the same copy of the Koran, as being strongly intermixed with Persian and Arabic), there is, in some cases, far more difficulty in deciding on the Indian or Persian origin of certain fabrics and manuscripts. Many miniature paintings in particular come from India, where they were painted by Persians, who being sectaries of Zoroaster, and emigrating before the invasion of Islam, settled in India under the name of Parsees.

As an example of a fabric Persian in manufacture and Indian in style, we may call attention to the chintz represented in Plate XX. which gives us an almost complete idea of the Indo-Persian flora in a state of semi-liberty. Large radiating flowers expand on twisted stalks, ananas, pinks, nuts, pomegranates, honeysuckles, poppies, daisies, flowerets of every sort, a whole botanical world, in short, peoples this composition, which is also animated by birds of all sizes, and even quadrupeds running along slight trailwork. According to M. Jacquemart, the representation of the peacock and fern fronds would show the origin to be exclusively Indian, which is not disproved by the hooked nose, the almond-shaped eyes, and arched eyebrows of the flying genii bearing the stamp of the Indian race.

To the resources resulting from this mixed style, the Persians added those of great manual skill and a most remarkable fertility. Damasceners, bookbinders, potters, embroiderers, miniature painters, emulated each other in taste and skill.

Persian carpets are still considered the finest in the world, dishes, vases and enamelled bricks from that country are still such models in taste, that European art seeks them out, and our manufacturers endeavour to equal them by imitation. The Persian damascenings determined the type of that style of decoration during the sixteenth and seventeenth centuries of our era, a period corresponding to the reign of Shah Abbas the Great, which terminated in 1628, and is considered to be the apogee of Persian art.

The various Indian, Arabian and Persian styles which have just passed in review before us, and which have already so many points in common, in respect to composition and forms, resemble each other particularly in the use they make of polychromatic decoration.

Thus the remark that we have already made on the subject of Indian productions, where no attempt at rounding-off the figures is to be found, is equally applicable to all Oriental productions.

The rule is a silhouette drawing with geometrical outlines relieved by conventional colouring on a dominant and generating ground. Attention to this rule produces brilliancy and repose, when the design is well combined and the colours happily chosen. The varied scales rise from the colour of the ground, either black, white slightly tinted, blue, red, yellow and flesh-colour, with mediums of isolation or union, varied according to the nature of the production, but always aided by flat tints, and with striking outlines of every shade from black to white, according to circumstances.

The Persians are especially skilful in this manner of treating and varying these ornamental resources, and from them the best lessons in decorative colouring may be obtained. (See the two carpets, Plates XXIII. and XXV. and the earthenware, Plate XXII. in which the prevailing colour is green, the favourite colour of Mahomed.)

The use of gold takes an important place in the bas-relief ornamentation of the Moors, in which the three primary colours, fused together by the judicious play of light on the paler parts, form the basis. (See Plate XXX.)

This use of gold is also interesting in the paintings of Plates XXIV. XXVII. and XXVIII. but its effect becomes altogether charming, as we see it in a constellated and *studded* state, scattered over the productions of the modern Indians. (See Plate XIX.) In the parti-coloured grounds, passing from black to white, from red to green, peculiarly Hindoo in style, changing colours with the design, which undergoes in its details a similar reversing of colour, the Indians succeed in neutralizing the most glaring intensities into a general harmony, by means of gold which, thrown over the rawness of the colours, seems to unite and warm and, as it were, blend them into one, like a transparent veil interwoven with gold.

BYZANTINE.

PLATES XXI. TO XXXVII.

E treat this important style apart, as not entering completely into any of our three great divisions, Ancient, Asiatic, and Western art, but serving as a sort of link between the two former, on the one hand, to a union of which it owes its origin, and the third, on the other hand, which it has long continued to inspire.

Byzantine art may, indeed, be considered as a product of the degenerate art of the Greeks, combined with that of the Asiatics. This union must have been occasioned by the conquest of a part of Asia by the Romans, who, becoming more and more curious in decorative magnificence, found in the East fresh elements to satisfy their sumptuous tastes. The exact nature of these elements, their character and importance, however, still remain very doubtful.

Before the time of Islam, which seems to have developed their genius as well as their power, the Arabs must have possessed an original art; but of this only a few traces remain in legends, in which grand buildings are spoken of, which go back to remote antiquity. In consequence of some catastrophe, perhaps an inundation, they are said to have come up into Africa and Asia, and to have founded several kingdoms in Syria, amongst others that of Hira, the architectural luxury and riches of which town form the object of marvellous recitals in these legends. (See Coste, "*Architecture arabe.*") It is moreover known that the wandering and stationary tribes called each other by the name of *Felt people* and *Clay people*, which indicates with respect to the latter the existence of keramics, the decoration of which is unknown, as well as that of their arms, their fabrics and fixed dwellings. We may conclude from these traditions that an Arab art of African origin was transplanted into Asia in consequence of some emigration of unknown date; that this art must have undergone modifications, of the importance of

Detail taken from the Church of Marmoutier.
(Byzantine style.)

which we cannot judge, on their contact with the Greeks as on that with the Indians and Persians, and must have formed an important part in the compromise called by the name *Byzantine*.

Subsequently, at a period posterior to the greatest time of Byzantine art, and under the influence of Islam, when Arabian art took the form under which we now know it, there may well have been, in some applications and in various points of contact, a certain Byzantine influence exercised on Arab practice;[1] but it would be an exaggeration to refer to Byzantine art, as is sometimes done, the very origin and formation of the Arab style, which has too much character and unity, not to be essentially, and in its principal lines, an original conception. The truth appears to be that there was a mutual

---

[1] See Notices of Plates XXXIV. and XXXVI.

influence exercised, as inevitably happens in this sort of contact; but that if the Arabs received anything in this exchange, it may be said that they were partly taking back their own from an art which had drawn so largely from Oriental sources, both in its first formation and also in the period of its greatest development.[1]

However this may be, an important place in the history of ornament belongs to the Byzantine art, which, after having united the two great Greco-Latin and Asiatic currents, spread on one side over the north-east, where it even now determines the style of Russian ornaments, and in the other

Byzantine Ornaments. (Theotokos Church, at Constantinople.)
(After Gailhabaud.)

into our west, where, combined with the peculiar aptitudes of nations of Celtic, Latin, and Lombard origin, it furnished the elements of the *Romanesque* style; and lastly, by a fresh contact with eastern art, at the period of the Crusades, took its part in the formation of the *Gothic* style.

The construction of ornament is less complicated with the Byzantines than with the Arabs. The logic in it is the same, but less carried to its full consequences; overlapping is far more rare, and in accordance with Greek principles it is generally satisfied with a single ground.

The palmate flowers spreading out from the stems, the generic form of which is immediately derived from the Greek vases, are precisely similar in their outline to those of the Arabian ones; but their indented design has not the fulness of that of the latter, and they have likewise fewer resources; but although the beauty of design in the details is not so great, the decorative effects are broadly conceived; and still show with advantage the influence of the Greek principles. In coloured Byzantine ornament, with simple well-ordered silhouettes, where the area of a generating ground is much more unembarrassed than with the Asiatics, there is always some repose for the eye. The foliage is refined, and the floral developments conform to the laws of nature. A flora in rich and ample forms sometimes assumes the highest decorative importance. See Plate XXXI. Nos. 31, 32; Plate XXXIII. Nos. 9, 14, 18, 19, 23, 24; and Plate XXXV. No. 4.

Border taken from a Book of the Gospels, of the eighth century.
(Taken from "*Arts au Moyen âge,*" by P. Lacroix. Paris, Firmin Didot.)

In this style, however, the variety is extreme, and under the union of two original arts we can perceive all the resources of individual effort and a knowledge of every style. We sometimes find a decorated ground, borders composed in the style of the Indians, and with only the floral ornaments employed by them: in these the richest effect is produced by a repetition of a single design by mere juxtaposition (see Plate XXXIV. Nos. 1, 3, 4, 6, 7, 8). Sometimes, besides the regular repetition which forms the rule, the Byzantines practise symmetry as understood by the Greeks, that is to say, produced by the equivalence of forces, and not by the mere repetition of the whole subject placed side by side or reversed (see Plate XXXI. Nos. 30, 32; Plate XXXV. No. 6).

---

[1] On the founding of Byzantium, Constantine had summoned Asiatic artists, and at a later time a great number (during the reign of Justinian) worked under the Greek artists, Anthemius of Tralles and Isidore the Milesian, at the construction of St. Sophia's, and the other monuments of the Justinian period, which in consequence bear traces of their influence.

The geometric arrangements of the Byzantines are most ingenious and especially remarkable in mosaics, the monotony of which they combat by well-conceived, complicated constructions. They depend usually on a play of the straight line and the right angle. For these constructions see Plate XXXIII. Nos. 1, 5, 6; Plate XXXVI. Nos. 13, 14, 15, 16, &c.; and Plate XXXVII. Nos. 7 and 23.

The Byzantine geometric mosaics are distinguished from the Latin mosaics by this construction forming an integral part of the design. Amongst the Latins, construction is in general exterior, that is to say, produced by means of architectural lines formed by mosaic work, which is nothing more than a filling up, executed with the simple square or triangle of rudimentary marquetry. We here give a few examples which will assist in explaining the differences. These fragments come from the church of St. Lawrence beyond the walls, at Rome; we take them from "*Monuments anciens et modernes,*" by M. Gailhabaud. M. Lenoir speaks of them in the following terms: "These fine

Mosaics of the Bishop's Throne, at St. Lawrence beyond the walls.
(After Gailhabaud.)

mosaics, hardly to be met with elsewhere than in Italy, presented great difficulties in execution, as much because they are laboriously incrusted in marble, as because, on account of the geometrical designs which they form and their small dimensions, they required extreme precision in the adjustment. This sort of work had great success during the twelfth, thirteenth, and fourteenth centuries, especially in all the Roman States; and certain churches, such, for example, as that of Orvieto, have some on

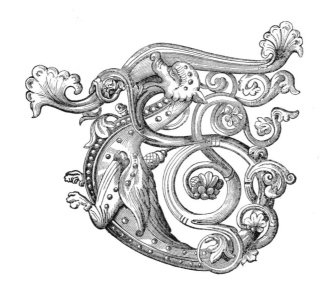

a part of their façades; the great cloisters of the churches of St. Paul beyond the walls, and of St. John of Lateran at Rome are covered with the richest designs executed in this manner . . . . . oriental pavements, which ancient authors called *opus Alexandrinum,* and which were in use in the churches of the East and of the West from the earliest ages of Christianity down to the middle ages."

The Byzantine design and, consequently, its colouring, are entirely *conventional.* A very feeble attempt at rounding off the figures may be noticed in the so-called Greek manuscripts and in the mosaics in Sicily, which are a direct imitation of the former. Everywhere else the artist proceeds by even tones simply opposed to one another on a generating ground, as everywhere in the East.

Amongst the Byzantines, ornament, properly so called, has no symbolic character, with the exception of the cross, which is multiplied under various figures, more or less differing from the historic type. However, we frequently find apocalyptic animals, and human or celestial figures bearing a religious meaning.

WESTERN ART.

I N considering Western art we must be guided by a chronological order instead of the ethnological one, which we have so far followed. We distinguish three great principal periods:—1st, the Middle Ages, 2nd, the Renaissance, 3rd, the seventeenth and eighteenth centuries, and particularly the history of French art during the latter period.

MIDDLE AGES.

CELTIC — ROMANESQUE — GOTHIC.

PLATES XXXVIII TO LI.

Celtic.

E have already said that Byzantine art, when spreading over the East, must have found amongst the nations of Celtic race, an indigenous art arising from the peculiar aptitudes of that race.

It appears, indeed, difficult not to perceive this character of originality in what is termed Celtic ornamentation, to which we have devoted two Plates, XXXVIII. and XXXIX. (see the notices on those plates), and of which the most remarkable monuments have been given in the interesting work of Mr. Westwood ("Miniatures and Ornaments of Anglo-Saxon and Irish Manuscripts"). This

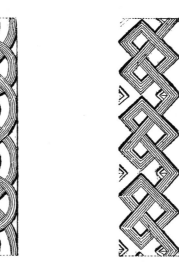

Celtic Interlacings.
(After the "*Monuments anciens et modernes,*" by Gailhabaud.)

author sets aside both the supposition of a Roman origin—contradicted by the difference between the regularly alternating interlacings of Latin mosaics with the knots of Celtic scrolls—and also that of a Byzantine origin, which would be disproved by the want of similarity between the early Celtic design and the ornamentation of St. Sophia's, as published by Salzenberg ; he draws a conclusion, then, in favour of the Celts having a spontaneous national art: leaving, however, undecided the obscure question as to whether it had its birthplace in Scandinavia or had come originally from Ireland, and afterwards spread through England, the Scandinavian Countries, and the North of France.

If we may be permitted to hazard an opinion on this difficult question, we should be inclined to decide between these two opinions, by going still further back and assigning an Asiatic origin to this art, similar to that of the Celtic race itself, which was a Scythian branch from the Aryan trunk, having penetrated by successive emigrations into the continents and isles of the north, and of which ethnological science has found the purest type in the Irish. In this way a common Asiatic origin, and proximity in a primitive state might explain a certain relationship between the Celtic and the Arabian processes with regard to geometric invention, notwithstanding a difference in the method of application which we shall have occasion to point out.

Without insisting more fully on this conjecture, which, whilst maintaining the independence of indigenous Celtic art with regard to Byzantine and Gallo-Roman art, would explain at once its original character and its simultaneous existence amongst several northern nations of common origin, we shall complete by a short description, the summary analysis we have given of this style in the notice accompanying Plate XXXVIII.

Interlaced ornaments form almost the only element of Celtic ornaments of the first period, and this alone would suffice to establish its antiquity, for intertwining is essentially a primitive method. Its distinctive mark is the division of the surface to be decorated by lines, the unrolling of which is frequently happy, always possible and logical. There is no doubt that the designs of these ornaments

Celto-byzantine Design.

Initial. (Celtic foliated.)

Celto-byzantine Design.

must have been procured originally from interlaced cords before they settled down into quasi-geometrical compositions. The pliability of the medium employed would procure the additional resource of spirals and curves instead of rectilinear angles, and this forms a characteristic difference between the Celtic and Arabian geometrical design. We are struck by the variety of the productions obtained from such simple elements; there is a real charm in following them through their complications, which sometimes attain to great depth, and prove by their skilful divisions, the clearness of the links, and the ingenuity of the windings and knots, a real understanding of ornamental construction.

There was wanting, however, a vital element in this style, and its resources were indeed threatened with exhaustion from having used every possible combination, when it obtained this necessary element of life from Byzantine art, with which it was afterwards brought into contact.

Mixed Period.—Romanesque Style. It is from the time of this transformation, or rather of this compromise between the two arts, the date of which may be fixed in the ninth and tenth centuries, the time of Charlemagne and his successors, and in which the originality of the two combined arts may easily be recognized, that the future superiority of the productions of western Europe is foreshadowed.

By appropriating the flora of Byzantine art, the Celtic ornamentalists soared to greater heights. They preserved a portion of their original interlacings; the other became the stem from which sprang leaf-work, and which terminated in floral expansions. Having thus obtained some real decorative richness, the Celtic style rose to the level of art. At the same time, the difference we have already mentioned between it and purely geometric conceptions, such as is usually found in Arabian decoration, became more striking from the more frequent addition of heads of quadrupeds and birds, serving as terminals to the principal lines, which thus are made to represent bodies elongated out of all just proportion or probability, from which emerge feet or claws corresponding with the head. Such as they are, these fantastic and grotesque images constitute a separate art, which interlacings alone could never have done (see Plate XXXIX. Nos. 13, 15, 16). Precisely similar ones are found on the sculptured stones of Great Britain and Scandinavia, which fact imparts to the old charters and missals, whence our polychromatic examples are taken, the interest of representing, under every aspect, an original and complete style.

In Plate XXXIX. we have inserted examples taken from the second and more fertile Celtic manner. The ornamental clasps and roses, Nos. 18, 22, are combined with the greatest force. The initials on an open space, Nos. 19, 20, 21, equal the best works in iron. The initials on a coloured ground, Nos. 34, 35, 36, 37, in their rich and well-ordered fulness, in which the two elements, Celtic and Byzantine, are happily balanced, are the most complete expression of this ornamentation of the tenth century. Vigour of design, skill in division, a constant logic, exfoliations and expansions in conformance with the general rules, are to be especially noticed in these compositions, as also the results of light procured by the delicate colouring which sets them off.

As in the east and amongst the Byzantines, the design and colouring are entirely *conventional;* only a very weak modelling can be noticed, which is merely meant to show the roundness of the stems or calices from which emerge heads or fresh branches, Nos. 19, 20, 21. No symbolic meaning appears to have been attached to the Celtic ornaments, except, perhaps, in the designs, so frequently found, without beginning or end, and which appear to be a symbol of eternity. (See Plate XXXVIII. Nos. 8, 18, 23, 24, 31.)

This union of the Celtic and Byzantine styles did not entirely give way to the Gothic style, with which it long co-existed.

It furnished the types for the finest ornamentation of glass and manuscripts, which, at this period—during the eleventh, twelfth, thirteenth, and fourteenth centuries, the most brilliant period of the middle ages—resembled stained glass on a greatly reduced scale. Even in the fifteenth century, direct traces may be found in Italy of the Celtic style in the marginal vignettes then in fashion (see Plate XLIII. Nos. 17, 18, 19, 20), and used concurrently with margins in the Latin style of the Renaissance.

Border taken from the Bible of St. Martin, of Limoges. (Tenth century.)
(Taken, as are the two other borders, from the " *Arts au Moyen âge,*" of P. Lacroix.)

Border taken from a Book of the Gospels, of the eleventh century. (Munich Library.)

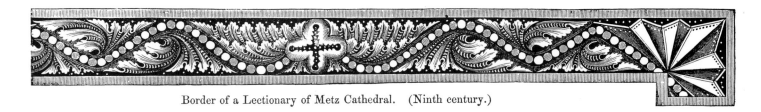

Border of a Lectionary of Metz Cathedral. (Ninth century.)

In the greater part of our plates which belong to the middle ages, we can trace the combined or isolated use of the two elements in this mixed style (Plates XL. to XLVI.)

Those examples which are of Latin or Lombard origin proceed more directly from the Byzantine. The Romanesque style draws more impartially from both sources.

Thus, No. 1 in Plate XL. is derived from both styles: the two corners on a purple ground are Celtic, as well as the parts of initials on a purple ground, Nos. 13, 14, 15, 16; the remainder are Byzantine.

The Scandinavian paintings in Plate XLI. as well as the enamels and fabrics, are of Byzantine conception.

In the glass represented in Plates XLIV. and XLV. the union or isolation of the two styles is also easily to be recognized; in Nos. 1, 19, 28 of the first, and Nos. 28, 29, and 30 of the second, their union may be easily perceived.

In Plates XLII. and XLIII. taken from manuscripts from Italy, where it is known that Byzantine art retained its sway longer than in the North of

A Capital; eleventh century.

Europe, although the former is plainly Byzantine, the second contains examples of the change that was taking place on the very eve of the great epoch of the Renaissance.

Pointed.—This style, long called Gothic, is now more frequently termed the *pointed style*, on account of the pointed arch in architecture producing its principal characteristics, even when applied to ornament.

The term *pointed arch* is applied to one " formed by two arcs of a circle of equal radius, which meet at their summit and form a curvilinear angle." (Batissier, " *Histoire de l'Art monumental.*")

Enamels on the front of the Altar of the Church of Comburg, in Germany. (Twelfth century.)
(Taken from " *Monuments anciens et modernes,*" by Gailhabaud.)

We shall merely remind our readers of the claims of which the invention of the pointed style has been the object. Interesting examples of the intersection of the semi-circle may be found at Mycene, in the Pelasgic tombs, and in some of the Roman monuments—amongst others, the aqueduct of Tusculum; and, applied more broadly, we find it at Cairo in the Mosque of Ebn Touloun, built in the ninth century under Persian and Byzantine influences; it may be found also in the course of the tenth century, amongst the Arabs in Sicily, from whence it is said to have passed into Neustria with the Norman conquerors.

The pointed arch, introduced into the North of Europe in the latter half of the twelfth century, was used there exclusively in the thirteenth.

Ogee of the Cloister of the Choir of Notre Dame at Paris.

In the first pointed period the use of the new style was confined to architecture. In it the pointed arch existed by the side of the Romanesque semi-circle, in the same way as it is found in Arabian buildings in the same monuments as the horse-shoe arch.

It was not at first employed exclusively; for during the Romanesque period decorations borrowed from former periods were used with it.

But before long, great numbers of fresh types of ornament sprang from this stem, and the artists of the North deserve honour for having extracted from this accidental form developments which rendered it almost a new creation. They framed laws for its general ordering and details, and formed that style, the almost exclusive use of which during three hundred years has covered with its wonders nearly the whole Western World.

An examination of Plates XL. and XLIV. will assist us in understanding the transition period between the first and second pointed styles. The first of these Plates still belongs, in the style of its ornaments, to the pure Romanesque. The second, of a later date, gives already some idea of the radical

Detail of Cologne Cathedral.

differences which were about to take place in ornament. (We give here a table of the numbers of Plate XL. to assist the study of this transition.)

The valuable manuscript of Luxeuil, from which the greater part of these examples are taken, belongs to the twelfth century, and offers a characteristic survey of the details of Romanesque decoration. The Celtic forms are here found side by side with the Latin manner, in the same way as architecture was already making use of the semi-circle and of the pointed arch.

Thus Nos. 26, 33, 54, 55, 56, 57, 58, are Celtic. The introduction of the new element is seen in the decoration of the columns, the whole of the shafts of which are ornamented with branches, scrolls

Details of the Ogee mentioned at page 34.

Plate XL.

Details of the Ogee mentioned at page 34.

and foliage (Nos. 15, 16, 37, 38), and the capitals of which (Nos. 47, 48, 49, 50), relieved by foliage, sometimes bend down their crockets from the top of the corbel, at others lean over from top to bottom, now alone, now united to the human figure, of which at other times (No. 51) an original use is made as a support of the column itself.

On the other hand, in the friezes and borders we find the Greek fret-work (Nos. 17 and 18), reversed zig-zags (No. 41), heads of nails hollowed out (No. 42), the teeth of a saw enriched with an alternating vegetable ornament (Nos. 30, 31), and in all the other examples designs more or less recalling the antique; heart-shaped leaves, ova, aquatic leaves, and rich plants, filling up the grounds without leaving any interval.

In this Plate then, with the subjects (Nos. 45 and 46) occupying the corners and Nos. 1 to 16, which are Byzantine or Celto-Byzantine from a contemporary manuscript, we find once more all the imaginary and exotic types of ancient conventional flora in their latest forms, which were soon to be replaced, in the Gothic period, by an indigenous flora.

In the stained glass represented in Plate XLIV. notwithstanding the fact that the outlines are still Byzantine, an abandonment of ancient principles in ornamental details is clearly manifest. What the isolated Celtic art, so firmly knit by the logic of its developments, gave promise of in the tenth century, has now attained its full maturity. The types of the known conventional flora are elaborated in a less restricted area, and its elegantly divided and widely-blossoming petals combine gracefully with the constructive scroll foliage frequently utilized to limit alternating grounds. Sometimes this constructive element is a bare twisted branch (Nos. 16, 38); sometimes the windings are double and the two branches cross each other (Nos. 6, 14, 36); there are some imbricated constructions (No. 35) and some forming a quincunx (Nos. 4, 8, 9, 10); combinations in which the floral element alone comes into play (Nos. 11, 24, 26), and braids (Nos. 22, 35) beaded or striped, and sometimes twisted like Celtic knots. The constructive elements intermingling with the floral ones, which frequently issue from it (Nos. 1, 15, 22, 35), divide or direct all their expansions.

The strict arrangement, the brilliancy and richness of the subjects chosen, the wisdom and variety shown in the divisions, the force of the deductions and the vigour of the design, indicate that these noble productions are the work of that hardy race which decided the superiority of Western Art.

From the close of the thirteenth century the ancient styles, some traces of which had lingered until then in the details of ornaments, entirely disappeared from architecture, where the pointed style ruled supreme, with some ingenious modifications which it would be beyond our limits to describe. We will not then enumerate the various sorts of arches, *sharply pointed, lancet-headed, stilted, wide, trefoiled, concave,* with a *cyma recta,* or a *cyma reversa,* and *elliptical,* which have been so clearly analyzed in the *Cahiers d'instructions* published by the " *Comité historique des arts et monuments,"* in 1846, and which since that time have figured in every treatise on architecture. We mention these although we have no time to dwell on them, because their outline is the generating principle of all the ornaments depending on it. A study of the stained glass, Plate XLV. proves this fully. The curvilinear forms arranged on the inflexible square form the basis of these fourteenth century designs, Nos. 1, 2, 3, 4, 5, 6, 7, 8, 9, 10, 12, 14, 15. In these examples the quatrefoils, trefoils and roses are obtained from these outlines, constructed as in architecture; the second ground

Details of Cologne Cathedral. (From "*Monuments anciens et modernes,*" by Gailhabaud.)

of great fulness, on which these constructions impress a coloured silhouette, is taken from geometric combinations, from Celtic interlaced designs and, as yet timidly, from the indigenous flora, to the exclusion of all antique remembrances.

This style of ornament is quite original, not only in its forms but in its principles. Nowhere

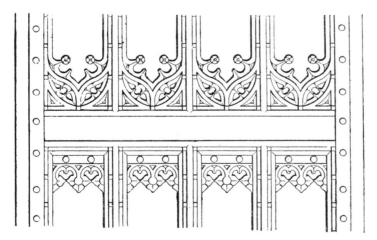
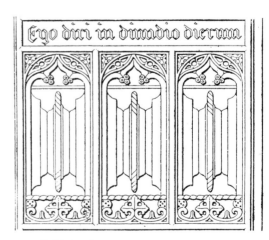

Sculptured Gates of St. Alban's Abbey. (From Gailhabaud.)

do thĕ decorations of details flow so directly from the lines of architecture. The constructive element of the ornament in Western hands is no longer a mere fiction, as in those of the Arabs, for example; it imitates the real building and adopts its forms; all its details follow naturally from the principles of the great architectural lines, so that the trefoil of a simple balustrade, or of the smallest panel may enable us to determine the age and style of a whole building.

The details of these ornaments, which vary from the most rudimentary to the most luxuriant caprices of the *flowery* or *flamboyant* style, assist in giving this idea of construction, without changing the nature of the ornament, by following the architectural line.

By the side of this monumental art, so severe in its logic whilst capricious in its smaller details, and of which stained glass, facings, enamels, tiled flooring, and sculpture in relief, on stones, wood or iron, were during the middle ages the principal and almost exclusive manifestations, there arose a beautiful branch of art, induced by observation and the sentiment of the *real,* and obtained by naïve imitation of nature, in those numerous manuscripts to which such value is now attached, and which take so important a part in the history of national arts.

Italy, the Low Countries and France possess the most curious specimens of this new art, which, by opening a wider and more varied field to painting in the domain of ornament, prepared the way for the great revival of the sixteenth century.

Manuscript miniatures which at first resembled stained glass transferred to parchment, or as Didron says, *cartons à vitraux,* afterwards produced a poetic work contemporary with the stone poetry of the cathedrals. Independence and simplicity form the charm of this commencement of picturesque ornamentation. In the fifteenth century the principal elements were obtained from flowers in which the indigenous species take a larger place than they had yet occupied.

The ivy, ivy grape, vine, cinque-foil, water-lily, buttercup, oak, strawberry, reed, mallow, cabbage, thistle, holly, endive, daisy, rose, pink, heartsease enamel the border of the manuscripts. (See Plates XLVIII. and LI.)

" By the side of digitate, palmate or ternate leaves, there twine around incised, lobed, sinuate and feathery forms" (see "*Instructions du Comité des arts et monuments* ") intermingling with simple branches or with fruits sometimes easily to be recognized, sometimes difficult to name. Now and then the butterfly and other insects are introduced to animate the floral world with their many-coloured tints, and ingenious combinations occur of ribbons in large folds (remains of the Celtic style) on which inscriptions are written.

A charming and inventive spirit animates this half fantastic, half real world, which pervades the foliage of the decoration, in which during the later periods, taste forms the only guide, as may be seen in Plates XLIX. L. and LI. which terminate this series of the Middle Ages.

Border of a Latin Book of the Gospels
of the thirteenth century.
(Taken from " *Arts au Moyen âge.*")

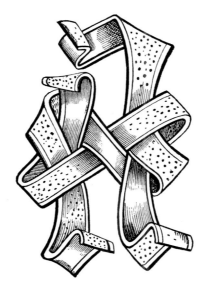

RENAISSANCE.

Plates LII. to LXXIII.

ITALY, even during the Middle Ages, never entirely lost the traces of ancient tradition towards which her very origin and her genius ever led her, although at certain periods she had only recognized this tradition through a Byzantine medium. The Italians had only to search among their ruins in order to bring the works of their ancestors once more to light. So, when literary enthusiasm impelled every mind so irresistibly towards the study of antiquity, Italy became the focus and active centre of the great artistic movement, usually called the Renaissance, which, by extending its influence over other nations, was to change the face of art.

This complex and fruitful movement we shall not undertake to describe: it belongs to the general history of the fine arts, and has been frequently related. We shall confine ourselves therefore to observe its influence from our special point of view and with reference to our subject.

Pendant after Benvenuto Cellini. (Cabinet of Antiques, National Library of Paris.)
(Taken from "*Arts au Moyen âge.*")

Here we shall find in all that relates to ornament, though with some inventions of fresh types, the impress of the highest genius in the use and application of the types borrowed from the antique, from the East and from the national arts of Western Europe.

The immortal phalanx of great Italian artists of the sixteenth century, who determined the definitive direction of Western taste towards a rejuvenescent ideal still more varied and full of life than the ancient art from whence it emanated, raised the decorative arts to the utmost, carrying into them that breadth of ideas and extent of knowledge on every subject which these masters owed to their thorough artistic education. Each of them being at once a painter, architect, sculptor, frequently an engineer, mechanician, engraver or musician, and always well read in general literature, found all his resources and means of execution in himself.

In such hands, ornament necessarily assumed a new character and extended its domain. It could not but abandon by degrees the more or less uniform types and formulas imposed on it by the almost exclusive ascendancy of architecture, or handed down by the practical tradition of crafts, and thus lead decorative art into the way of a relative liberty already thrown open to it by the fancy which had characterized the close of the Gothic period, especially in the illumination of manuscripts.

At the same time the science of design, perfected by contact with the finest models and freed from the simplicity and inexperience of the Middle Ages, favoured in the compositions of this period a large introduction of the human figure, which by its presence determined the proportions of the surrounding objects.

Ornament from this time was frequently united whilst remaining subordinate, to the plastic arts, which had now reached their greatest perfection, and by which it was carried forward in the path of progress.

The Italians, then, during their *golden* age rendered decoration a superior and universal art.

Before the complete formation and definitive development of the style of the Renaissance, a certain number of Italian ornamentalists of the fifteenth century preluded this revolution in art by compositions, which may be considered as a transition stage between the style of the Middle Ages, and that of the sixteenth century.

Leaf scroll, of the fifteenth century.

Plate LII. represents in this style some of the work of Girolamo da Cremona. Its strongly conceived ornaments are evidently inspired by the rich forms of Roman sculpture. A massive flora and colouring and design tinged with something of wildness, are its peculiar marks. The combinations exceed the ordinary domains of manuscript illumination of the fifteenth century. The books from which our illustrations are taken are indeed of a size which brings them nearer to fresco decorations. The Antiphonals and Graduals, some containing anthems, others masses with notes, are choir books, and in the cathedrals of Sienna and Florence, and the Carthusian church of Pavia, there are some which are upwards of four feet in height.

The principal subjects in Plate LVII. (Nos. 1 to 11), have also been taken from manuscripts painted by Gherardo and Attavante, celebrated Florentines. The style is more finished than that of the paintings in Plate LII. The ornamentation is everywhere of a well-sustained richness and elegance; it consists of finely drawn branches, tastefully winding, usually taking the forms of the acanthus, and frequently terminated by an expansion of rose-work resembling in some degree the botanical type. Figures of children, pearls or cameos frequently relieve these decorations; a style which is seen in Nos. 3, 4, 5, of Plate LV. in paintings attributed to Giulio Clovio.

Raphael gives us the highest expression of Renaissance ornament. Many others preceded him; but as M. Dumesnil says ("*Art italien*") "he arranged, harmonized, transfigured all that came before him."

It was with the assistance of Polydore da Caravaggio, a skilful ornamentalist and painter in grey, and of Giovanni da Udine, who excelled in the painting of fruit, flowers and animals, that Raphael covered the walls of the Vatican with the decoration from which we have taken the subjects represented in Plates LIII. and LIV. and Nos. 12 and 13 of Plate LVII. as well as the engraved ivories (Nos. 1, 2, 3, 4, 5, of Plate LVI.) treated after the same designs. This ornamentation was imitated from that of the ancients, a specimen of which had just been brought to light by the discovery of the Baths of Titus, and which was afterwards confirmed by the excavations of Pompeii and Herculaneum, of which the genius of Raphael seems almost to have had a presentiment. The master's hand is particularly noticeable in the panels representing the four Seasons and the three Fates; the judicious and sure taste of the *divine young man* is to be found everywhere.

Such decoration gives a high idea of the domain of ornamental art, and shows how extensive should be the knowledge of those who aim at such a noble ideal.

Besides this fine restoration of antique modes, brought about by Raphael and his school, there also ensued a distinct and important fact which it is necessary to mention. The artists of the sixteenth century, after having reconstructed the ornament of the ancients, experienced the need of adding to it resources of greater variety in the details, and of providing fresh elements suited for larger decorative effects. The greatest glory of the Italian Renaissance is perhaps the invention of these additional ornaments. The *volute scroll*, substituted for the leaf scroll, or combined with it, was the novelty

Volute Scroll. (Period of Francis I.)

of the period; cartouches, of which a far more important use was beginning to be made, soon appropriated the *double volute* in relief, and this style, thus enriched by a fresh element, took an entirely original

Volute Scroll. (Period of Henry II.)

development. Moreover, this new element was so logical that it was adopted by the greatest masters in architecture, and since that time has passed through every modification of taste, never ceasing to take a part in the greater number of modern decorations, whilst the fashion spread even into the most minute ornaments.

The history of the cartouche still remains to be written. By grouping in separate Plates those that we have been able to collect, according to their chronological order and the successive modifications they have been subjected to, without counting the considerable number of minor examples which are to be found in other Plates, we have endeavoured to render some real service, by giving the landmarks of a study necessary to all ornamentalists. (See for the sixteenth century the special Plates LVIII. LXXI. LXXII. and the general Plates LIX. LX. LXI. LXIII. LXVII. and LXIX. which contain some examples.)

Volute Scrolls, with examples of Volute in Relief. (Period of Charles IX.)

The first cartouches of the sixteenth century belong to what may be called the age of wood; they have the appearance of carved wood; the natural rolls of fine shavings made with the plane are perhaps its true origin.

The foliated volute scrolls were made into elements of ornamental construction similar in their aim to those of which the Arabs had felt the necessity, but endowed, like the stems of plants with which they were combined, with the curve and grace of the classic foliated scroll.

Volute Scrolls. (Period of Henry II.)

In this style the bareness of the outline of the constructive foliated scrolls is agreeably inter-mingled with the indented vegetation of the scrolls of the acanthus family, which was brought into honour again by the Renaissance. In this intermixture the breadth is atoned for by the lightness of the outlines of the foliage, and also by the open work which facilitates overlapping. The use of plat-bands in these foliated volute scrolls, variable in their length, renders the presence of figures of all sorts reposing in them or apparently passing through, more probable. Masks, ribbons, flowers, or fruit, correct too great a severity by offering some points of repose in the general distribution. Either alone or combined, these elements of ornamental construction, corresponding in so many respects with the ancient traditions of western logic which we have stated, have been perhaps the principal agents in bringing about the most valuable manifestations of modern European art.

With them, the broad and ever-recurring acanthus stem of the Romans, or the ornamental vase from which hung down or ascended doubly twisted branches along the frieze and panels, no longer pre-vailed exclusively. Great numbers of free or imitated cartouches form the basis of fresh develop-

Cartouche with volutes in relief, 1556. (Printer's mark.)
(Taken from the "*Arts au Moyen âge*" of P. Lacroix.)

ments, and the use of engraving in the hands of the best artists occurring at the same time as these new modes, caused the rapid spread of the style, and propagated examples of it everywhere. In the Netherlands, Germany, France, Italy, England, and Spain, arose similar conceptions, the local origi-nality of which constantly increased its domain.

The further we advance into the sixteenth century the more do we see that the antique element, the restoration of which had been the first effort of the artists of the Renais-sance, however weakened by the dispersal of the Roman school after the death of Raphael, became mixed with other elements drawn from different sources and combined by modern genius in conformance with its own instincts. Already the name *Arabesques*, given to the decorations around the paintings in the Loggie of the Vatican, had attested a certain consideration for Eastern fashions, which the commercial activity of the Italian Republics afforded means of knowing and applying. The Arabian outlines exercised a certain influence on the design of the new scrolls, and the purity with which, during the sixteenth century, the Venetians employed the Persian manner (See Plate LXVIII.), leaves no doubt as to their perfect acquaintance with the Oriental style and their appropriation of it.

We have already reminded our readers that the artistic movement of the Renaissance was not confined to the frontiers of the country which had given it birth. From Italy it speedily spread amongst other nations, and every art of native growth, of local or original nature, was more or less modified through this invasion of Italian art, the effects of which were long and durable.

In the North, after the death of Albert Dürer, the style of which he was the most remarkable representative was not continued after his immediate pupils, and the Netherlands, which had been, during the fifteenth century, an artistic focus rivalling that of Italy, lost in a great degree during the sixteenth, the powerful originality which had distinguished it.

In France the Italian style exerted no less influence, and the French artists were drawn along like the others by this irresistible current.

The results of this revolution, which undoubtedly raised the standard of art, have been variously judged. If we remember, that the French nation was already in possession, especially in regard to decoration, of a simple and original art, which was tending towards further development, and also that at the time when the excess of Italian artists spread themselves over Europe, and especially into France, where they were invited by the kings, they brought with them a facile taste, and a practice already far removed from the finest times of the Raphaelesque Renaissance, and representing a period which, notwithstanding their personal merit, was already to some extent a period of decay, we can under-stand why modern criticism, more just than that of an earlier time towards the centuries preceding the age of Leo X., which are now more studied and better understood, should have expressed some regret at this sort of confiscation of French national genius, thus arrested in its natural course. But was not this in-evitable? could the art of our ancestors have existed without modifications whilst it possessed so powerful a neighbour, and not seek to profit by the progress made in the science of design and the search after a higher ideal? The simplicity and close resemblance to nature which form its special attraction, but which in part were owing to real inexperience, would have lost their charm by becoming less unconscious and

Design taken from the Charterhouse of Pavia, after Gailhabaud. (Italian Renaissance.)

Decorative Design attributed to Jean Cousin. (French Renaissance.) (Communicated by M. A. F. Didot.)

Design taken from the Charterhouse of Pavia, after Gailhabaud. (Italian Renaissance.)

Decorative Design by Jean Cousin, taken from his "*Livre de Perspective.*" (French Renaissance.)

more voluntary. Almost every progress in art, however real it may be, is obtained at the detriment of a certain native vigour, which we cannot see lessened without regret; but the human mind cannot turn back, and must force its way through transformations which have always some degree of reason at the time at which they appear.

Amongst the subjects of French origin which we give in this part of our collection, some are contemporary with the best times of the Italian Renaissance, if not anterior to them (see Plates LVIII. LXIV. and LXV.); others, of a later time, bear the more visible impress of the Italian style and of the appropriation made of it by French artists, Jean Goujon, Jean Cousin and Ducerceau at their head. (See especially Plates LX. LXVI. LXVII. LXIX. LXX. LXXI. LXXII. and LXXIII.) Two of these (Plates LXXI. and LXXII.) are devoted to cartouches, the origin of which we have endeavoured to trace, and which were especially suited to the clear, logical genius of the French nation.

Volute Scroll. (Period of Henry III.)

SEVENTEENTH AND EIGHTEENTH CENTURIES.

PLATES LXXIV. TO C.

THESE two centuries derived their greatest brilliancy from France. Four distinct phases occur in them.

The first, characterized by the union of the Flemish and Italian styles, embraces the reigns of Henri IV. and of Louis XIII.; the second terminates with the seventeenth century, amongst the greatest splendours of the reign of Louis XIV.; the third comprises the close of the latter reign and that of Louis XV., during which period ornament fell, through over-care, into an excessive mannerism, until the revival of the taste for the antique, induced by the discovery of the bronzes and decorative paintings of Pompeii and Herculaneum, which discovery was the principal instrument in the formation of the Louis XVI. style, filling the last period.

Although it was during these two centuries that the French schools shone with the greatest brilliancy, after having profited by the Italian Renaissance and appropriated it to themselves, we must go much further back to trace the history of the influence of French art inscribed in more than one durable monument unanimously recognized by modern criticism.

From the Middle Ages, indeed, through her geographical position, which explains the contact of the different currents of ideas coming from the North and the South, and through the power of assimilation which characterizes her judicious and observant genius, France had become the centre of an artistic production which was commendable by those master qualities of French art, moderation, sobriety, correctness of drawing, and clearness of conception.

We may here be permitted a rapid retrospective glance over those first fruits of French national art, which the necessity of not interrupting the history of the Italian movement and its influence obliged us in that place too much to abridge.

During the Gothic period, the priority in which belongs to France, where the greatest number of its monuments are to be found, that country was, from the thirteenth century, highly renowned for its statues and stained windows, and her artists, scattered through Europe, carried their style into Germany and England, where it was highly appreciated.[1]

After having given to the world the spectacle of a "grand, audacious, deeply calculated architecture," as Emeric David says, an architecture which had been unequalled since the finest times of Greece, the thirteenth, fourteenth, and fifteenth centuries brought forth crowds of painters, sculptors, gilders,

---

[1] Germany, whilst placing her powerful impress on the productions of Gothic art, kept closer to the French type than England. The latter, after having long had French and even German instructors, marked by a peculiar stamp the elliptic arch of the Tudor style. Nowhere else is anything to be found similar to this style, which is of Venetian richness. It is impressed with an entirely national character, of which the English are justly proud.

and glass stainers, having schools in every provincial town, and practising their arts in the whole of France, with local varieties: a marvellous preparation for the restoration of antique tradition which the Italians were coming there to install.

The fact is now acknowledged that in all those active centres known by the name of Parisian, Picard, Lorraine, Tourangel, Norman, Breton, Burgundian, Gascon, and Southern schools, in which vigorous artists were developed, Italian art was quickly understood and applied, soon becoming absorbed and transformed by the French mind with a success which the schools of Bruges and Cologne, frequently successful rivals of French art during the pointed period, were not destined to equal.

Then, when in Italy the magnificent blooming time at the first half of the sixteenth century was already passing away, even before the close of the century, through the excessive facilities indulged in by the artist, France, introduced to fresh elegances, which she had entirely appropriated to herself by bringing to bear on them her own native qualities, regained for herself a place which her experienced genius had previously occupied. Jean Goujon, with the elongation of his beautiful figures of nymphs, came nearer to the Greeks than any of his contemporaries, and Jean Cousin, skilful in all the arts, adorned with his innumerable compositions glass, canvas, the vellum of manuscripts, the pages of printing, goldsmith's work and pottery, with a science and sureness of taste which have caused him to be looked on as the true founder of the French school.

Details of the Church of Saint Etienne du Mont at Paris.
(Seventeenth century.)
(Taken from the " *Monuments anciens et modernes*" of Gailhabaud.)

The old schools of the North transformed, by which we mean those of Flanders, the Rhenish provinces, with that of France at their head, maintained then, better than even Italy herself, what Fra Giocondo, Leonardo da Vinci, Il Rosso, Primaticcio, Andrea del Sarto, Benvenuto Cellini, Serlio, and Paul Ponce Trebati, had taught them.

Those schools, already so rich in architects such as Jean Bullant, Philibert Delorme, Pierre Lescot, and afterwards Ducerceau, whose vigorous ornaments come entirely within our subject, mark by their own genius the masterpieces of engraving of those who were called the *little masters*, such as Etienne Delaune, Théodore de Bry, Virgile Solis, Aldegrave, Woeriot, &c., who in the seventeenth century were represented by Jacques Mestre, Etienne de la Belle, Michel Blondus, H. Janssen, &c. &c.

As far as their works are engravings, they are beyond our subject, but their goldsmith's work, which for the most part has not escaped destruction, bears witness to a genius too original to allow us to pass it by in silence. Historically the productions of these artist-engravers and goldsmiths, as those of potters, locksmiths, cabinet-makers (some in the middle of the sixteenth century, others at its close and at the commencement of the seventeenth), prove that the level of ornament was maintained in the North at a height to which it no longer attained in Italy, then filled with the mannerism, which inferior imitators of the sublime but contorted style of Michael Angelo had brought into vogue, and the sight of which, it is said, troubled the end of that great man. It thus prepared the way for those twisted decorations, the convenient and lax principles of which were in the next century to produce in France the Louis XV. style.

The glorious memory of its *golden age*, however, still gave it influence, and caused a superiority to be attributed to it which was only justified in its past.

Pendant of Gilles l'Egaré.
(Eighteenth century.)

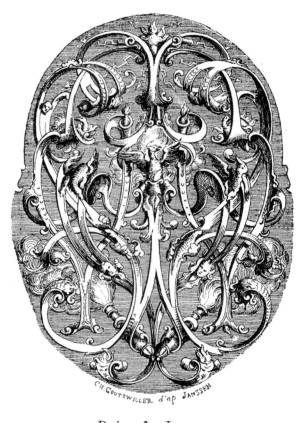

Design after Janssen.

Embossed gold Cassolette. (French work of
the seventeenth century.)
(Taken from "*Arts au Moyen âge.*")

This was seen clearly when, at a later time, under Louis XIV. Bernini, who was then enjoying a European reputation, came into France, whither he had been summoned by the king to finish the Louvre. His arrival was hailed with delight, but he was soon sent away overwhelmed, it is true, with gifts and caresses; after having seen him at work and in conflict with the equally stately but substantial genius of the French artists, the public were undeceived.

About the close of the sixteenth century and the commencement of the seventeenth, the independent character, which energetic and original artists had preserved in the application of the principles brought into honour at the time of the Renaissance, went on decreasing to make way for a closer but more timid imitation of the direct models of antiquity, which were becoming more abundant, and exciting general admiration.

Thence ensued, assisted by the troubles of the time, a relative sterility; for, according to the expression of a modern critic (Guilmard, "*Histoire générale de l'ornement*"), "antiquity was ill studied at that time; artists had rather the wish to imitate it than the ability, and they were far from comprehending its true power and exquisite purity."

We must add that, after the errors of the Italian artists employed under the later Valois, it was to a certain degree a happy re-action, which caused the return of art to the common source. After these attempts, beginning with such stilted elegance though not devoid of delicacy, we perceive in it a sincere love of the antique, and also that it was contemporary with the elevated and thoroughly French style of Nicholas Poussin. Nos. 2, 3, 4, 5, 6, 7, of Plate LXXIV.; the ceiling of the Louvre and the fragment of a panel from Fontainebleau (Plate LXXVI.) are the results of a return to the principles of Roman antiquity; for that was almost the only antiquity then thought of.

Yet, in the arabesque decorations of the apartment of Marie de Medici in the Luxembourg, Plate LXXVI. the freedom of the Renaissance time is once more felt; it is a last ray from the Italian influence of the favourite Concini.

Conjointly with this more or less frank return to the mode of the antique, there took place in the decorative arts a movement which was at first favoured by the victories and reign of Henri IV., and which also took an important part in the formation of the style predominant during the reign of Louis XIII. and the first part of that of Louis XIV. The fashion then turned towards Flemish productions. The variations these productions passed through may be studied with advantage in the collection of ornaments engraved between 1607 and 1624, and their peculiar character may be recognized in the series of our plates.

Whilst preserving some remembrance of the Italian Renaissance, the new foliated scrolls (see Plate LXXVI.) of manuscript and enamelled ornaments, and also the cartouches, piers and escutcheons (Plate LXXVII.), make up, with Plate LXXV. sufficiently varied examples of the new style, whose tendency to heaviness could not fail before long to become somewhat excessive.

The style of the first part of the seventeenth century finds its most complete and happiest expression in the compromise of Nos. 1 and 4, in Plate LXXVII. We shall not dwell on the strangeness of the forms of the cartouches with which the rest of the plate is filled.

The Chinese productions, of which Holland was at this period the principal *entrepôt*, must have greatly contributed to arouse, or, at all events, to keep up a taste for the representation of objects of this nature, the principal merit in which is their elasticity; for they will adapt themselves to every need and will form any combination. The Italians, although they made use of them, did not dare to carry them so far.

Pendentive taken from the Frescoes of Annibal Caracci in the Farnese Palace.

The success of these inventions is principally owing to the master cabinet-makers, who, like the Flemings Vriese and Christopher Feinlin, or Frederic Unteutsch, of Frankfort, executed or engraved so much furniture of a heavy magnificence, which has again been copied in our days.

Cabinet-making, so much developed by the manufacture of these magnificent cabinets and chests, in fashion during the Renaissance, and specimens of which have come down to us, shows that the Germans,

French and Italians were equally skilful and ingenious in this manufacture, and cabinet-making seems indeed to have been the special ground on which the transformation and union of styles took place.

Neither goldsmith's work nor painting had indeed any occasion for the sometimes exaggerated amplitude to which recourse was had by the *workers in wood*, at that time well-educated men.

When, after the summons of Richelieu and the " discomfiture of the famous and unique Monsieur

Frieze after Lepautre.

le Poussin, the honour of the French in his profession, and the Raphael of our age," as a contemporary says (see N. Destailleur, " *Notices sur quelques artistes français*"), Jean Lepautre was called upon to a certain degree to direct the taste of the period, he came from the workshop of a cabinet-maker, where

Designs for Cartouches after Lepautre.

he had been early placed as an apprentice. It is true that this workshop was no other than that of Adam Philippon, who styled himself " cabinet-maker and engineer in ordinary to the king" (towards the close of the reign of Louis XIII.), and who had been sent through the whole of Italy to seek "the most celebrated men in the arts of painting, sculpture and other professions necessary for the decorations of royal palaces, and had brought into France great numbers of workmen and of the finest bas-reliefs and antique figures." This may show the importance of such cabinet-makers, and the knowledge concealed under so modest a title.

It was from this journey in Italy, in which Philippon must have been accompanied by his pupil that Lepautre returned, with his taste formed, and in a position to produce those numerous and varied works, with such gorgeous decorations, which represent the most brilliant period of the Louis XIV. style.

The lessons which he brought from Italy were no longer those of the pure and elegant school of Raphael. Long before this time Giulio Romano, at Mantua, and the other pupils of Raphael in the rest of Italy, had exhausted in some degree the arabesque style, the tendencies of which, more and more tinged with the picturesque, had rapidly degenerated.

When Lepautre was in Italy, and numerous workmen were induced to leave that country for France, Bernini was reigning at Rome; but what was of greater importance was that it was immediately after the glorious time which the school of the Carracci, founded at Bologna at the close of the sixteenth century, had restored to Italian art. When all the other schools were in a state of decay, this Bolognese school returned to the best traditions of decorative art (see p. 59), and it was principally from it that the pomp-loving and fertile Lepautre was to receive his inspirations. Nothing, indeed, could have been better suited to his taste than the grand and vigorous style, occasionally verging on inflation and excess, of the Italian decorators of this school.

The nature of the decorative ornaments of the school of Lepautre does not allow us to bring them into the subjects that we have treated in colour. Conceived with a view to broad effects, and somewhat of the nature of stage-painting, they are too unlike what is required of modern arts and

Frieze after Lepautre.

manufactures for an ordinary use to be made of them in anything but architecture, for which they were intended.

Notwithstanding the passionate admiration which then prevailed for the antique, artists could not touch it without altering and overloading it, for it was considered too grave and bare. They wished to give it greater richness, and in trying to perfect it changed all relations of proportions with an exaggeration, a *furia*, of which the accompanying friezes will give some idea.

The desire to make everything grand was the stumbling block of that time. Its best result was a powerful effect of unity, owing principally to the great designers, the architect Mansard and the painter Lebrun, the latter of whom did indeed possess the necessary authority to direct the decorative arts of every kind. An artist in every branch of art like the great Italians, but an absolute despot, he presided over everything that was to be done : " sculptures, ornaments for the interior of apartments, tapestries, goldsmith's work, iron-work, mosaics, tables, vases, lustres, candelabra, all passed through his hands, and nothing appeared at the Court that was not invented by him and executed under his directions." (Louis and René Ménard, " *Tableau historique des beaux-arts.*")

The incredible quantity of public and private buildings, which seemed to arise almost spontaneously, at this time, gave to the France of Louis XIV. a general character very different from that of the preceding times. In the north and south, east and west, we find everywhere the well-known type of that architecture, not without grandeur, but which, by sacrificing everything to magnificence of appearance, frequently accords but ill with the object proposed. The necessity of decorating buildings promptly and simultaneously in so many places, while stimulating the whole industrial world and forming an incalculable number of workmen, could not but cause a great laxity in the choice and execution of details of every description.

The peculiar originality of each of the provincial schools disappeared in this general movement, in which each individual could only make use of types promulgated by the central academies. Unhappily the forms employed, being of too easy choice and design, sometimes weak, singular, twisted and heavy, disfigure this ornamentation, which, although sustained by the greatest energy, fatigues the eye by an overcrowding of detail.

What distinguished France in the use of these over-decorated styles, at a period in which the Italians were doing still worse, and the rest of Europe was endeavouring to follow in their steps, resulted from the old habits of correctness and discretion which form a national characteristic. The level of the teaching was maintained by the great institutions commenced by Richelieu, encouraged by Mazarin and supported by Colbert. The direction of the artists of the Louvre, who produced works of superior excellence in every branch of art, and the power of education possessed by every master in his guild, contributed to give an exceptional value to the whole, notwithstanding a certain defect in the principles.

Running Ornamentation.   (Seventeenth century.)

The fault that we have indicated in the architecture of the time, was to be seen in everything; the sentiment which should inspire the use of decorative art according to the particular purpose of each object, was entirely wanting. There was now only one character of ornament for all objects, manufactured without sufficient thought of the special character required by their different destinations.

However, we must not forget that the acquired knowledge was great, and, although they sometimes changed the nature of what they borrowed, yet they knew how to turn it to account. Oriental processes, amongst others, were not without influence on the ornamentation of which we are speaking. They were used judiciously according to the forms in fashion; to the influence of the oriental earthenware must be attributed the geometrical conventional designs, with free colouring, the scallop decorations, with light foliage, or with a full surface, which form the ground of the earthenware, Plate LXXXII. The ideas for the tapestries of Plate LXXXIII. are also taken from the same principles; and whilst speaking of these tapestries, in which brilliant colours arranged with doubtful taste produce such confusion, we must call attention to the fact that Nos. 1 and 2 contain a remarkable example of design that is rich in instruction. It is a composition formed almost entirely of elements, whose combinations are infinitely varied without changing their nature ; the crossings in relief of the roses, canopies, cartouches, vases and bouquets, foliated constructive ornaments from which springs the acanthus, either covering them or striving away from them, clasps formed by neighbouring branches, finally the curves produced by different bits of branch-work having a common termination and resulting in an incidental figure, are all represented in these decorations of such characteristic make.

Again, the applications of Boulle work, Plate LXXXIV. are executed according to the sound data

Running Ornamentation.   (Seventeenth century.)

furnished by the Orientals as to design for surfaces.   The examples on Plate LXXXV. emanate directly from them ; the foliated volute scroll, No 4, Plate LXXXI. and the leathers on Plate LXXXVI. belong to the same series.   The divided and richly ornamented palm-leaves which appear several times in the last-

Tail-pieces.   (Bérain's style.)

mentioned plate would alone suffice, if placed near the works of the ancient Greeks, to give an exact idea of the process of enriching employed at that period.   These palm-leaves, with the elements mentioned above, give the whole history of running ornaments of the Louis XIV. style, in its usual applications.

The most brilliant, or at least the best-known representatives of this phase of French art are Jean Bérain and Daniel Marot.

The former was much in fashion and, although we may entertain some doubt as to the taste displayed in compositions where many grotesques occur, they at all events show much imagination.   In the decorations of the *Salon d'Apollon*, Plate LXXIX. in which he drew his inspiration from the pyramidal combinations of Raphael, making use at the same time of every resource of learning, we cannot fail to perceive that he has all the suppleness of a real talent, and that these works possess high merit.

Daniel Marot, whose imagination was not less rich than Bérain's, while his design was more elegant, and who was well fitted for the highest employments, was not, like Bérain, made designer in ordinary to the King of France.   This artist was a Protestant, and, being obliged in consequence to leave his native country after the Revocation of the Edict of Nantes, he went to Holland, and afterwards to England with the Prince of Orange, where he was named architect to that prince when he became William III.   The collection of 260 plates published by him in 1712 bears witness to his remarkable talent and fertility. His versatile power applied itself to everything : beds, chairs, armchairs, tables, mirrors, candelabra, large clocks, designs for tapestries and housings, patterns for fabrics, in short, says M. Destailleurs, "all the thousand objects of everyday life from the kettle to the hand of a watch ;" without counting the fact that, like Bérain in France, he was the arranger of festivals and organizer of the grand funereal pomps which he has engraved.

The productions of Robert de Cotte, Gillot, etc., represent the latest formula of the Louis XIV. style. In the tapestries on Plates LXXXVII. and LXXXVIII., fresh elegancies may be felt. In the border Nos. 1, 2, 3 of Plate LXXXIX., a more careful execution, better detached details, a more sober treatment of the background, mark an improvement in taste, a little disfigured, however, by grotesque cartouches with barbarous figures, intended to serve as points of repose.

Emblematic Cartouche. (Seventeenth century.)

Under equally transitory forms, this style is also seen in the rich decoration with a gold ground in Plate XCI. as well as in the fine paintings in half camaieu of the well-arranged ceiling of Plate XC.

As we advance we see the tendency becoming more marked towards a light colouring for the ground of decorations, which becomes at last quite general.

Louis XV. Style.—The first change which ornament underwent, about the twentieth year of the eighteenth century, and which constitutes what is called the Louis XV. style, was commenced principally by the architects Gilles-Marie Oppenord and Juste-Aurèle Meissonnier, while the most complete expression of it is to be found in the works of Babel and Baléchou.

The origin of this transformation may be seen both in the excessive adornment which had prevailed under Louis XIV., and also in the example and success of Francesco Borromini, architect and sculptor, who worked at the cathedral of St. Peter's under the direction of Bernini, and died in 1667, after having excited great admiration by his broken lines, executed with remarkable facility and power of invention.

If, notwithstanding the glory of such a precedent and its chiefly Italian origin, France has had the honour of giving to this new style the name of one of her kings, which name has since been adopted everywhere, even in Italy, it is because the French school in adopting processes which tended to the overthrow of all the principles of order known until then, succeeded in giving to the liberty of form which she took up a stamp of lightness, grace and wit which are frequently wanting in the Italian and German productions of the same period.

It was not without difficulty that the new principles, or rather the overturning of all principles believed in until then, succeeded in finding acceptance. The vigour of the struggle caused in France by this invasion of new modes impelled their advocates to fresh efforts. Never were more address, ingenuity and real learning brought into the service of more doubtful doctrines.

After having abandoned all the old methods for which, says Cochin ironically "they had a superstitious respect," there remained no guide but personal taste, of which everyone had to give proof. Now, if notwithstanding the dangers of such a liberty, the honours of the century remained with the innovators of the time, it was because the artists who were protesting in favour of wiser principles were far from being equal to those who were pleased to fall in with the mannered style which soon became prevalent.

The mistakes caused by these vagaries, when they were tried by inferior hands, soon became excessive and before long such a state of decay was reached, that it was indeed time for the Greek antique to re-appear with her immortal youth through the shroud of lava which had preserved her.

However dangerous, when looked at in the light of general principles, may have been the independent and bold action of the school which produced the real brilliancy of the decorations of the eighteenth century, we cannot fail to acknowledge that it endowed France with some charming works of art ; that under the apparent frivolity of this art, and through its thousand caprices, we may discover a perfect understanding of the requirements of private decoration, which plays so large a part in modern life; an understanding which, by the force of example has not been without healthy influence on the decorative arts in our days.

Running Mouldings. (Eighteenth century.)

Besides this we must not forget that this art succeeded that of the first days of the eighteenth century, the time when Gillot, and after him his pupils—amongst whom was Watteau—had recourse to light decorations of capricious improbability in their details. From this point of view, the types of the new school, contorted though they were, yet at all events possessed the advantage of being more in conformance with the traditional and national habits of logic.

It may then easily be understood how it was that with such good qualities, the new manner, notwithstanding its defects, should have triumphed over the numerous criticisms it provoked; of which criticisms the engraver Cochin constituted himself the passionate exponent in the "*Mercure de France*," but some of which would now appear exaggerated.

Time indeed, although condemning certain abuses, has not ratified all the prejudices of the criticism of that period, of those, for example, who declared that "a candlestick should always be straight and perpendicular, to bear a light, and not twisted as if it had been forced." The skilful artists of the best period of the eighteenth century have long ago been joined by eminent connoisseurs in refuting what there was too uncompromising in such criticism.

To sum up, this century, with its boldness and skill is one of the most curious in the history of ornament. Its success besides was quite exceptional.

The superior arts, brought down to the same level of simple decoration, rendered it active assistance. After the fairy-like scenes of Watteau, so delicately drawn and warmly coloured, came the pearly-grey

Empyreans, and the pastoral pieces with a blueish landscape, of the erotic Boucher. These were objects of great value to ornaments intended for the mounting of pier-glasses.

Thus ornamentalists, whose art came in a manner to occupy a preponderating position, taught with an authority which their art, when secondary, had denied them.

After Oppenord, who, having studied ancient architecture, and worked at the Church of St. Sulpice, only joined with some reserve in the new movement, Meissonnier, who styles himself painter, sculptor, architect, designer of the bedchamber and cabinet of the king, gives us under the title of " *Architecture universelle,*" a collection of ornaments of his own invention, the object of which was to urge forward the impulse given to decorative art by Lepautre and Marot. This is what the sarcastic and somewhat unjust Cochin styles, " a gay architecture, independent of all the rules of what was formerly called good taste." (See on this subject the very interesting documents published by M. Destailleur, in his " Notices " on some French Artists.)

P. E. Babel, designer of ornaments and goldsmith at Paris, who understood the *Rock-work* style, better than any one else, also prided himself on furnishing models for architecture.

We should have been astonished at such an encroachment on the territory of the architect, if the liberal education of these ornamentalists did not explain, though without always excusing some of their pretensions. The celebrated goldsmith, Thomas Germain, made at the same time plans for buildings and

Moulding. (Eighteenth century.)

for pieces of plate; it was he who furnished designs for the new church of St. Louis of the Louvre, built in 1738, on the site of the ancient collegiate church of St. Thomas.

An analysis of the productions of that time in which every artist set his own stamp of originality on his works, forming differences which modern publications have endeavoured to point out, does not appear to us to come necessarily within the limits of our subject. All the ornaments of that period, whether they be by Meissonnier, Babel, Baléchou, Jean Daniel de Preissler, La Joue, Isaïe Nilson, Cuvilies, Jean-André Thélot, Jérémie Wachsmuth, François Xavier Haberman, Jean Léonard Wuest, Jean Léonard Eysler, Jean Hauer, Charles Roettiers or A. Masson, are all treated in a picturesque style, frequently agreeing but indifferently with the laws imposed by the decoration of surfaces.

Thus the principal result of the ever-increasing part performed by painting in decoration was to substitute for the *conventional* representation of objects, the *imitative* representation of which we spoke at the commencement of our essay as an eminently modern proceeding.

As a general characteristic of this style in form, we may notice an almost complete absence of straight lines, which are replaced by the curves of the letter S, and a contempt for every form precisely square, round or oval; and yet the style is treated with some grandeur, of which Meissonnier was the happiest representative.

The *rock-work* style which was to make its way into all the decorative arts, appears to have arisen from the art of creating artificial gardens, which were much in fashion even in the sixteenth century. We do not know who invented them, nor to what origin they may justly be attributed. The Chinese very frequently make use of rock-work in their gardens as well as in their decorations, and it was probably to those enemies of symmetry that the eighteenth century owed its large use of this decorative element, which stamps with so peculiar a mark the productions of the Louis XV. style.

However this may be, the French artists were the principal authors of the models in this style, which the immense collections of Hertel and Engelbrecht contained, and which delighted all Europe.

Plate XCIII. contains in the double character of its cartouches, the latest ornaments in the Louis XIV. style, by artists who persisted in ancient errors, and also others in the extravagant fancy of those belonging to the fashionable school. Nos. 2, 3, 12, 13, are by Bernard Picard; who was working at Antwerp between 1720 and 1730. No. 1 was painted in Paris in 1740. Nos. 4 and 5,

which still possess some symmetry, though without a straight line, present combinations and foliated scrolls of the intermediate time. No. 9, by Isaïe Nilson, and 10 and 11 by La Joue, belong to the best times of the *rock-work*. In these latter figures, as in that of No. 8, in the same plate, and in the mounting of the fan, Plate XCVI. we find use made of shells and endive, so fashionable at that time that the acanthus had almost disappeared.

The danger of these mannered compositions, retained in fashion

After Cuvilies.

during a certain time owing to their being executed with extreme skill, which made use of every material with unequalled dexterity, could not be long concealed when the execution fell into less skilful hands. After having created numbers of charming vignette painters such as Hubert Gravelot, Eisen, Laurent Cars, J. Ch. Lebas, Cl. Duflos, Choffart and Aug. de Saint-Aubin, the Louis XV. style was destined to disappear before the revival of antique studies, although it found representatives until 1789, and passed through all the excesses of a bad taste, some idea of which may be formed by the subject represented above.

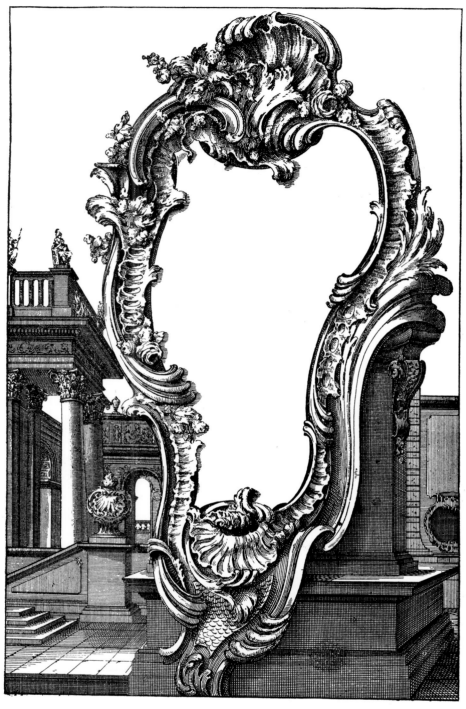

Cartouche after Babel.

After Cuvilies.

After Cuvilies.

Louis XVI. Style.—Even before the reign of Louis XVI. the return to a simpler taste had numerous partizans.   The discovery of Herculaneum in 1706, occupied people's minds even before the excavations presented results of any extent or real utility, which only happened about 1750 ; the re-action, then commenced in architecture by Servandoni and his pupil De Vailly, was not long in producing some effect in the modes of decorative art, and it was this same re-action which only attained a definitive formula under Louis XVI. whose name it still bears.

Rockwork Cartouche.

The works of Reisner, Gouthière Demontreuil ; " *Les lambris d'appartements, tant en peinture que sculpture,*" by De Neufforges ; " *Les sculptures, menuiseries, orfévreries et fontes,*" by De Lafosse ; " *Les décorations en peintures de fleurs et d'ornements,*" by Ransom ; " *La joaillerie et la bijouterie*" by the younger Pouget ; " *Les chandeliers et lustres,*" by Forty, as well as the compositions of La Londe and the charming foliated scrolls of Salembier, represent the varied expressions of the Louis XVI. style, interesting examples of which may be found in Plates XCVI. XCVII. XCVIII. XCIX. and C. ; (see the notices accompanying these plates) and which have lately been deservedly admired by amateurs.

Although here we bring to a close our short sketch, as well as our collection of illustrations, on the threshold of the revolution of 1789, it is not because we set no value on the efforts made in our own age, the fecundity of which is amply proved by the results obtained in the various branches of decorative art during late years, and which will, we hope, be still more firmly established.   But the time has not yet arrived either to judge impartially the work of the nineteenth century, or, still more, to recognize its definitive character through the successive infatuations which at first prevailed, or the wide eclecticism which has succeeded in our own day.

The first steps were especially difficult and obstructed in France. There the political agitations and long wars destroyed at once both the aristocracy of enlightened amateurs, and, what was still more serious, the workmen and artists formed by the good old French traditions, who were led by enthusiasm and want of work to the battle-fields of 1792, from which few returned.

The century had thus a two-fold task before it : to create public taste anew, and to re-establish centres of study ; neither of which could be the affair of a day.

Knowing this, it is no longer surprising that France should have spent much time in groping her way towards the light ; seeking it first under the Empire in a return to the antique, then in the pointed style during the Restoration and the literary movement of 1830, at a later time in a partial return to the decorative styles of the seventeenth and eighteenth centuries, and still more recently in a fruitful study of the productions of oriental art.

But, out of these various attempts and the lively discussions they occasioned, there has arisen in our time a wider, more enlightened, and more judicious appreciation of past ages.

After Salembier.

Numerous publications have brought before us the history of art, and this archæological erudition has enabled us to re-link the chain of broken traditions.

Modern art, thus freed from all exclusiveness, may, with a full knowledge of the facts, examine the works of the past, and make a choice from amongst the riches accumulated by our predecessors.

After Salembier.

Without neglecting the resources and variety of modern art, such as the sixteenth, seventeenth, and eighteenth centuries have bequeathed to us, furnishing as they do such excellent models of decoration, and as a whole, perfectly suited to our manners, modern decorators are able to find elements of strength and originality in that study of free and vigorous proceeding, of that high conventional decoration, which give so much character to the works of antiquity, to oriental and Asiatic products, to the stained glass of the thirteenth and fourteenth centuries, to the enamels of Limoges, and to the earthenware and majolica wares of the Renaissance.

In these they will find that power of effects which arises from freedom of colouring and a field always open to invention or to idealization, which raises the character of the artist's work and allows one of the masters of modern art to give this true formula of decorative art: "Ornament," says M. Guillaume, director of the School of Fine Arts (" *Idée générale d'un enseignement élémentaire*"), " must not change the form of the surface it decorates; it is on this surface, and either forms a part of it or is applied to it; it must not appear either to penetrate into it, or to be capable of being easily detached from it. . . . . *It is a very ideal form of art.* The ornamentalist, still more than either the painter or the sculptor, looks upon the art of design as serving to represent not real beings, but objects of an organism at once superior and dependent."

We feel certain that the present school, brought up with such principles, will make fresh progress

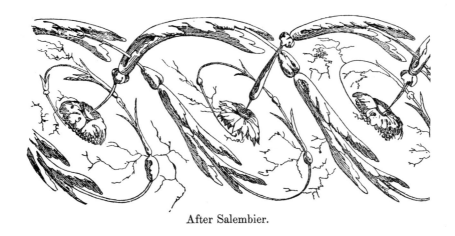

After Salembier.

in the road pointed out by the recent Exhibitions, and will find in the study of the best times, not a temptation to servile imitation, or to a simple copying, but models fitted to inspire original productions which may serve as models in their turn, and provide materials for a future history of the decorative arts of the nineteenth century.

PLATES AND DESCRIPTIONS.

PRIMITIVE ART.

WOVEN FABRICS, SCULPTURES, AND PAINTINGS.

The examples in the accompanying plate, although derived from very different sources, are connected with civilisations which are in some respects analogous.

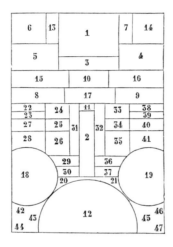

MUSÉE DE LA MARINE, LOUVRE.

Nº 1.
Woven fabric. (Oceania.)

Nº 2.
Woven fabric. (Central Africa.)

Nº 3.
Plaited vegetable fabric. (Central Africa).

Nº 4.
Braided fabric. (Oceania.)

Nº 5.
Braided leather. (Central Africa.)

Nᵒˢ 6 to 12.
Paintings in intaglio on wooden utensils. (Central Africa.)

Nº 12.
Round fan made of coloured feathers. (Oceania.)

Nº 13.
Border of a utensil of painted wood. (Central Africa.)

Nᵒˢ 14 to 17.
Paintings, ornaments on canoes and utensils. (Oceania.)

Nᵒˢ 18 to 21.
Painted decorations on Peruvian utensils, taken from *Antiguedades Peruanas por don Mariano Eduardo de Rivero y Dr. don Juan Diego de Tschudi.* — *Viena,* 1851.

Nᵒˢ 22 to 47.
Paintings on Mexican manuscripts. (Bibl. Nat.)

Lith. par Dufour & F. Ducin

Imp. Firmin-Didot.fr. Fils & Cie. Paris

EGYPTIAN ART.

DECORATIVE PAINTINGS.

The principal objects employed in Egyptian ornaments belong as a rule to the language of hieroglyphics.

Thus, for instance, the pink sphere with hawk's wings (N° 6) represents the rising sun. — The water-flowers intertwined with reeds in the lower part of the plate (N°s 4, 5) are types of running water. — The scarabeus, the black colour of which is so striking (N° 12), symbolizes immortality. — The running ornaments (N°s 10, 11) of which the Greeks afterwards made Vitruvian scrolls, signifying the rolling of the waves of the sea, is likewise a part of the language of Egyptian artists. — Red, blue, and yellow were the principal colours they used, with black and white to define the outlines; green was used more particularly as a local colour, for the stalk and part of the flower, though in the more ancient paintings blue is frequently substituted for it.

N°s 1, 2, 3.

Painted bouquets.

N°s 4, 5.

Grounds, borders, and bases from Thebes.

N° 6.

Painted sculpture, from the Memnonium at Thebes.

N° 7.

Undulating friezes.

N°s 8, 9.

Painted sculptures. — Little wooden columns.

N°s 10, 11.

Undulating friezes.

N° 12.

Ceilings.

Taken from the publication of the French Commission on Egypt and Egyptian Art, by M. Prisse d'Avesnes.

Lith. par Pralon.   Imp. Firmin-Didot fr. Fils & C.ie Paris.

EGYPTIAN ART.

JEWELLERY.

« Tombs », says M. Auguste Mariette, « sometimes become true historical monuments through the quantity of objects placed by the side of the dead. In them are to be found the objects which form the basis of all collections : amulets, statuettes of the gods, jewels, papyri, etc.

It is from cemeteries that those perfect specimens of Egyptian jewellery have been obtained which are so interesting to those engaged in ornamental work.

The broad and inflexible character of Egyptian design, which is so well expressed in metal, is especially suited to the work of the lapidary, and we ought to congratulate ourselves on the custom which required that every dead body should be adorned at least with its principal necklace.

Nᵒ 1.

Naos or breastplate of *cloisonné* enamel, with a tablet below the frieze bearing the name of Rameses II, XIX Dynasty. — Louvre.

Nᵒ 2.

Frame-work of gold, filled in with glass. — Louvre.
Both these jewels come from the Serapeum of Memphis. (The Serapeum is the mausoleum of Apis. Thus the god of the Serapeum, that is to say Serapis, is merely Apis dead. — Aug. Mariette.)

Nᵒ 3.

Scarabæus of lapis-lazuli with wings of glass beads. (The scarabæus with the Egyptians was the symbol of immortality.)

Nᵒ 4.

Necklace from the head of Apis.

Nᵒˢ 5, 6, 7.

Bracelets of *cloisonné* enamel.

Nᵒˢ 8, 9.

Rings opened out.

Nᵒˢ 10 to 26.

Ear-rings, necklaces, and amulets.

Nᵒ 27.

Sphinx taken from a stela, composed of the androcephalic lion. (The symbolism of the sphinx has not yet been sufficiently elucidated. According to the Greeks it symbolized strength both physical and intellectual.)

Nᵒˢ 28 to 33.

Jewellery from paintings at Thebes. Published by the French Egyptian commission, and M. Prisse d'Avesnes. (*Monuments égyptiens*, 4 vols. folio ; Paris, Didot.)

Lith par Candon & Durin.

Imp. Firmin-Didot fr. Fils & Cⁱᵉ, Paris.

PL. III.

ASSYRIAN ART.

EXAMPLES OF POLYCHROMATIC DECORATION.

Two distinct periods may be remarked in Assyrian art : the first, that of the foundation of Babylon by the Nabateans, on an alluvial ground destitute of stone quarries — a period characterized by the exclusive use of brick, and when the architectonic system was consequently forcibly restricted ; — afterwards a second period, that of Nineveh, founded by the Scythians, the conquerors of primitive Babylon, in a region where basalt and numerous stone quarries rendered possible a monumental architecture which the Babylonians had not known.

It is in general to this Ninivite period, which might be called the Scytho-Assyrian, that the remains collected in the museums of London and Paris belong.   The various specimens given in our plate belong to this period.

NINEVEH. — PALACE OF KHORSABAD.

N° 1.

PAINTED SCULPTURES, Layard.

N°s 2, 3, 4.

PAINTED SCULPTURES, Victor Place.

N° 5.

BRICKS INLAID IN COLOURS, Layard.

N°s 6 to 10.

ENAMELLED BRICKS, Victor Place.

N°s 11 to 18.

VARIOUS SPECIMENS, Layard.

N°s 19, 20.

PAINTINGS, Victor Place.

N°s 21 to 23.

RESTORATIONS, by Botta.

PERSEPOLIS.

N°s 24 to 33.

RESTORATIONS, by M. C. Texier (l'Arménie, la Perse et la Mésopotamie. 2 vols. folio; Firmin Didot).

Dufour & Lebreton lith.

Imp. Firmin-Didot, fr Fils & Cⁱᵉ Paris.

GREEK ART.

CONVENTIONAL FLORA, FRET-WORK OR MEANDERS.

The conventional Greek flora is very far from being a representation of any species of plants. It adopts merely their general characteristics; the types are varied but slightly, and the painted ornaments on architectural monuments are precisely of the same nature as those of smaller proportions on vases. Several of these representations, however, resemble nature; the laurel, ivy, vine, and aloe are easily recognized.

We give examples both of the flora of Magna Græcia, and of the same flora treated with greater freedom on the vases of Apulia.

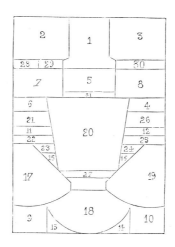

N° 1.

Painted antefixæ. Temple of Jupiter Panhellenius, at Ægina. (Blouet, *Expédition scientifique en Morée*, 3 vols. folio; Firmin Didot.)

N°s 2, 3, 4.

Terra-cotta ornaments from Athens. (Le Bas, *Voyage archéologique en Grèce et en Asie Mineure*; Firmin Didot.)

N°s 5, 6.

Paintings from vases, published by Hittorff.

N° 7.

Paintings from vases. From the Campana Museum.

Paintings on vases, taken from the Gewerbehalle.

N°s 13 to 16.

Ova of ogee, with undulating friezes.

N°s 17 to 20.

Paintings taken from figures of Apuleian vases published by Gerhard.

N°s 21 to 30.

Fret-work or meanders. (The Greeks made use of waves or meanders to distinguish water from land.)

Lith. par Dufour & Mathieu.

Imp. Firmin-Didot fr. Fils & Cie. Paris.

GREEK AND GRECO-ROMAN ANTIQUITIES.

SPECIMENS OF POLYCHROMATIC DECORATION.

The accompanying plate contains numerous specimens of polychromatic decoration taken from various periods of Greek Art, dating from the time of the monuments in Ægina, or the Parthenon, down to that which may be called the Greco-Roman. The colouring is taken from drawings by the most competent artists.

The following is a list of the subjects in our plate, with references to the authorities on which our information is based.

Nos 1, 2, 3.

Frieze and corona ornaments, from the restoration of the Parthenon, by M. Paccard. (École des Beaux-Arts : Roman section.)

Nº 4.

Ornaments from the frieze of the temple of the Wingless Victory at Athens. (Lebas, *Voyage archéologique en Grèce et en Asie Mineure*, I, pl. 8, Nº 1.)

Nº 5.

Ancient fragment from a panel of a corona. (Lebas, id., II, pl. 6, Nº 1.)

Nº 6.

Antefixæ from the temple of the Wingless Victory. (Lebas, id., I, pl. 6.)

Nos 7, 8, 9.

Ancient fragments from different monuments at Athens. (Lebas, id., I, pl. 8, Nº 4; II, pl. 5, Nos 1 and 11.)

Nº 10.

Decorations over the entrance to the temple of Minerva Polias at Athens, from the restoration of that monument by M. Tétas. (École des Beaux-Arts : Roman section.)

Nº 11.

Frieze ornament on the temple at Pæstum, from the restoration by M. Thomas. (École des Beaux-Arts : Roman section.)

Nos 12, 13.

Ornaments on the temple of Jupiter Panhellenius, at Ægina, from the restoration by M. Garnier. Exterior (12); Interior (13). (École des Beaux-Arts : Roman section.)

Nº 14.

Star from the Propylæa. (Lebas, Hittorff, etc.)

Nº 15.

Cymatium, forming a gutter, found among the ruins of a temple at Metapontum. (*Métaponte*, by M. le duc de Luynes et F. S. Debacq, pl. 7.)

Nº 16.

Face and soffit of an ornament in earthenware, serving as a covering to the beams, found at Metapontum. (Id., pl. 8.)

Nº 17.

Painted mouldings. (Hittorff, *Architecture polychrome chez les Grecs*, pl. 9, fig. 10, p. 767.)

Nos 18, 19.

Vitruvian scrolls.

Nos 20, 21.

Meanders.

Nº 22.

Painted ornaments on a sarcophagus found at Girgenti. (Hittorff, *Architecture polychrome*, pl. 9, p. 767.)

Nº 23.

The coping of a wall and ceiling in the temple of Nemesis at Rhamnus. (Hittorff, id., pl. 10, fig. 9, p. 768.)

Nº 24.

Fragment of mosaic-work found in Sicily. (Hittorff, id., pl. 5, fig. 5, p. 761.)

Nos 25, 26, 27, 29.

Interlaced ornaments. (Greco-Roman style.)

Nº 28.

Meanders. (Greco-Roman style.)

Nos 30, 31, 32, 33.

Ornaments in terra cotta found at Pallazolle (Hittorff, id., pl. 7, fig. 1, 2, 3, p. 764), with the colouring given by the same author in his restoration of the temple of Empedocles. (Pl. 2.)

Nº 34.

Ornaments. (The same restoration, pl. 3.)

Nº 35.

Palm leaves.

Lith: par Dufour et Sanier.

FIRMIN-DIDOT FRÈRES, FILS & Cie ÉDITEURS.

Imp. Lemercier & Cie Paris.

ETRUSCAN ART.

JEWELS.

All the objects represented in our plate belong to the Museum of the Louvre; the greater part are in the Campana Collection and some of the most interesting were found in a tomb discovered by MM. Noël des Vergers and François at Vulci. The most ancient among them do not appear to date further back than the later period of the Roman Republic. In the specimens given here Greek and Egyptian influences are noticeable, the latter being especially visible in the frequent use of the scarabeus.

The fibula formed of a hand with ring and bracelet, and terminating in the form of a serpent, is considered to be Greek.

The intaglio in the centre of the bezel of a ring (N° 2), which is also capable of being used as a seal, appears to be of the same origin.

Ear-rings are considered to be the master-pieces of Etruscan jewellery. The kind called *à selle*, a specimen of which may be seen in the subject representing a child suspended, in the upper part of the plate on the right hand, belongs to the best period.

The necklace (N° 1) is reduced to one half the size of the original. N°s 2 and 3 are rings opened out. N°s 4 and 5, represent heads of hair-pins. N°s 6 and 7, represent ear-rings reduced in size. The hand of Venus holding the apple of Paris is probably Greek.

In some of the objects, of which the use is uncertain, the influence of the later Byzantine and Gothic periods may be recognized, and it is therefore doubtful whether they can be attributed to the Etruscans.

GRECO-ROMAN ANTIQUITY.

POMPEIAN STYLE.

DECORATIVE ARCHITECTURE.

It is far less to the domains of reality than to those of fancy that this purely decorative architecture belongs, which we find in the inner walls of the apartments in Herculaneum and Pompeii. Tradition attributes to the painter Lidius, in the time of Augustus, the invention of these architectural compositions, so elegant though improbable, whic hare frequently intermingled with maritime scenes and landscapes, or animated by various figures. They were executed by Greek artists, or by Etruscans working under their influence, and gave great delight to the Latins who did not seek in them the forms of their own architecture — characterized especially by the use of vaulted ceilings and arcades — but the elegance and poetry of the Greek art, by which they were so much captivated.

The principal subject of the plate is a painted wall from the *Casa delle Suonatrici*, taken from the great work of Zahn : *Les plus beaux ornements et les tableaux les plus remarquables de Pompéi, d'Herculanum et de Stabiæ; Berlin*, 1828-30. It is considered one of the finest of its kind.

The two single figures have been added to the design, but they do not exist in the original. One of them, that of the dancing girl on the dark ground, was discovered in the *Torre dell' Annunziata*. It is the finest of the twelve figures which were found in the same apartement and is one of those which Pliny calls *Libidines*. — The little winged genius, with Bacchic attributes, which occupies the upper medallion, was found at Cività.

These two figures are taken from the great work of Mazois : *Les ruines de Pompéi* (4 vols, folio; Firmin Didot).

Lith. par Sulpis & F. Durin.

Imp. Firmin-Didot fr. Fils & Cie Paris.

PL. VIII.

GRECO-ROMAN ART.

MOSAICS, PAINTED BAS-RELIEFS, AND MURAL PAINTINGS.

		6		
16				17
		7		
11	8		9	11
		20		
	14	5	15	
3		12		4
	1		2	
18			19	
8		13	10	

The use of mosaic is very ancient; its name is derived from the Greek word Μοῦσα, Muse.

« If an invention », says M. Barré, « is attributed to the Muses collectively, and not to some particular artist or special divinity of the second rank; if that invention has never become the theme of the narrations of poets and fabulists, we may be sure that it has been a common practice from time immemorial, and comprises nothing that might be called a discovery. »

(Herculanum et Pompéï, by H. Roux and Barré. — Paris, Firmin Didot.)

It is difficult to determine precisely the periods in which the Greeks, and after them the Romans, passed from the use of simply decorated pavements to mosaics with figures.

All that we know with any certainty is that the taste for mosaic pavements was only developed amongst the Greeks under the Asiatic influence of the successors of Alexander.

According to a passage in Pliny, we may believe that mosaics of artificial crystals, used for the imitation of painting, first appeared at Rome about the time of Vespasian. (See the passage quoted from M. Jeanron in the introduction.)

The specimens contained in our plate may be thus divided :

Nos 1 to 7, mosaics found at Herculaneum and Pompeii.

No 6 from the House of the Faun, and no 7 from the House of Polybius, both at Pompeii.

Nos 8 and 9 represent painted bas-reliefs at Pompeii.

Nos 10 to 20, are taken from panels, friezes, borders and mural paintings.

All these specimens are reproduced from the great works of Zahn and Mazois.

Jetot, lith.   Imp. Firmin-Didot fr. Fils & Cie, Paris.

CHINESE ART.

MEANDERS AND SCALLOPS.

The specimens contained in the accompanying plate are taken from vases in bronze incrusted with tin, silver, or gold, in the possession of the Baroness de Rothschild and Messrs. Burty, Evans, Laurens, and Mentzer; some are modern, others of the highest antiquity. All were exhibited at the *Exposition Orientale,* organised by the *Union centrale des arts appliqués à l'industrie* in 1869.

The greater number are represented in the illustrated catalogue, in 42 folio volumes (Bibl. Nat.), of all the vases formerly contained in the Imperial Museum of Pekin, a great number of which were unfortunately destroyed at the sack of the Summer Palace. This loss is to be regretted from an historical as well as from an artistic point of view, as many of the vases were manufactured in commemoration of historical events, and thus served as memorials of facts and dates, as has been stated by M. Stanislas Julien.

This great Chinese scholar, when exhibiting a sketch of one of these vases, the inscription on which proved that it was offered to the emperor Wen Wang, 1200 years before our era, *i. e.* about the time of the siege of Troy, asserted that there were some even more ancient.

From the ornamentalist's point of view few studies are so interesting as that of these spirited meanders, so different, notwithstanding their similarity of style, from the Greek meanders with their lineal rigidity. These ornamental constructions, the symmetry of which is so ingeniously varied, give a high idea of the decorative art of the ancient Chinese, and are capable of numerous applications in modern decoration.

Bauer, lith.

Imp Firmin-Didot fr. Fils & C.ie Paris.

CHINESE AND JAPANESE ART.

CLOISONNÉ OR PARTITIONED ENAMEL.

We have ventured to unite under the title of Chinese and Japanese the various specimens of enamel collected in our plate. They do in fact belong to one and the same style, as the art of ornamentation in Japan was formed under the influence of the Chinese and presents no special characteristic to account for the esteem in which its productions of are held, other than perfection of workmanship and superiority of individual taste.

If it is difficult to distinguish, in this *genre*, what comes from China, and what from Japan, it is frequently still more difficult to decide whether any particular piece belongs to ancient or to modern times. A few connoisseurs may distinguish them by the method of their manufacture or the use of certain enamels; but the system of ornamentation has in general remained the same and has changed the less from the circumstance that the most recent productions are merely copies of ancient ones. M. Jacquemart, in his *Merveilles de la Céramique*, speaks thus on the subject :

« The Chinese are most skilful forgers and they speculate on the taste of their fellowcountrymen for ancient and valuable works. It has happened in China, as with us, that the talent of imitators has succeeded in giving to their works a reputation and price equal to that of the originals. »

CHINESE.

Nᵒˢ 1 to 4.
Collection of M. Ed. André.
Exposition Orientale of 1869.

Nᵒˢ 4 to 11.
Manuscripts from the Bibl. Nat.
Cabinet des Estampes.

Nᵒˢ 12, 13.
Collection of M. Dutuit.
Exposition Orientale of 1869.

Nᵒˢ 14, 15.
Manuscripts from the Bibl. Nat.

Nᵒˢ 16, 17.
Collection of M. Baur.
Exposition Orientale of 1869.

JAPANESE.

Nᵒˢ 18 to 21.
Collection of M. Cœrli Dugléré.
Exposition Orientale of 1869.

CHINESE.

Nᵒˢ 22, 23.
Collection of M. Monbel.
Id.   of M. Dutuit.
Exposition Orientale of 1869.

In plate the ornaments are on a green ground and consequently the effect of the whole is rather dull. Here the frequent use of blue grounds and sometimes of yellow, black, white, and red ones tends to give the whole a more brilliant aspect. Nᵒ 23 is an example of pierced *cloisonné* enamel.

Lith. par Durin.

Imp. Firmin-Didot fr. Fils & Cie Paris.

JAPANESE ART.

CLOISONNÉ ENAMEL.

Amongst the productions of this highly decorative Eastern art, the Japanese style occupies a position that forbids us to pass it by in silence.

We give an interesting specimen of it in the accompanying plate, which contains a number of examples all taken from the same object : a copper dish in *cloisonné* enamel decorated on both sides. The upper part of our illustration is occupied by a portion of the whole work, separate details of which are grouped in the lower part.

Japanese art, although very ingenious in the employment and combination of geometric lines, does not confine itself to that alone. The figures of flowers and animals are also treated with much purity, and it is to be noticed, that the interior divisions, which are unavoidable from the very nature of the work, always leave the outline of the object distinct.

The colours are like those of the original in the relative value of the tones, but are rather less dark as a whole; it was thought that a greater degree of freshness and brilliancy would, probably, better represent the original state of the model, and, at any rate, would make it a more useful object of imitation for modern art. (See Ch. Burty, *Émaux cloisonnés, anciens et modernes*, Paris, 1868.)

Lith. par Painleve   Imp. Firmin-Didot fr. Fils & Cᵢᵉ Paris.

CHINESE AND JAPANESE ART.

SILKS AND RUNNING PATTERNS.

The silk which forms the principal object in our plate is one of the finest examples of the decoration of woven fabrics that it would be possible to study.

Yellow — the colour which Ziegler calls the « eldest daughter of the light » — forms the ground : it is the livery of the reigning dynasty of the Tai-thsing in China. The dragons with fours claws, which ornament it, would at once indicate to the Chinese the rank of the person for whom it was destined.

« The emperor, » says M. Jacquemart (*Merveilles de la céramique*), « his sons, and the princes of the first and second rank, bear as their attribute a dragon with five claws. The princes of the third and fourth rank bear the same dragon with four claws; whilst those of the fifth rank and the mandarins have for their emblem merely a serpent with four claws, called *Mang*. »

It may be noticed in this fabric that the effect is obtained, not by gradations of tints, but by abrupt opposition of colours, and that the white separating outline enables the eye at once to grasp the design; these outlines are so narrow as to be tinged by the neighbouring colours, with the exception of the white surrounding the dragons which is wider, and in consequence more intense and luminous, and, as it were, creates an atmosphere in which the monsters move.

We have endeavoured, by graduating the tint of the ground, to imitate the play of the silky fabric under the action of light.

This piece of silk covers a Chinese book in the *Cabinet des Estampes* of the Bibl. Nat.

The specimen on a black ground in the lower part of the plate is Chinese; the small ones at the sides on a black ground and all the others are Japanese.

Jetot lith.

Imp. Firmin-Didot fr. Fils & Cie. Paris.

PL. XIII.

CHINESE ART.

FREE DECORATION.

On the green ground in the upper part of this plate is a specimen of the ornamentation in which Asiatic taste revels in complete liberty, utterly regardless of the mutual relations of the objects represented. The combinations and oppositions of tones are extremely fine. The bold touches of intense red-brown, and the occasional use of black, successfully prevent all dulness, and give to the ground-work an appearance of aerial lightness.

The pattern on the ground of yellow ochre is a fragment of embroidery in which the gradations of effect are more boldly given, and in which there is generally more vigour. It is a perfect model of the style, and we may notice in it that it is by the white outlines — an unexampled method of isolation — that the design conquers the overwhelming strength of the ground and stands out with the requisite firmness and relief.

Lith. par Durin.   Imp. Firmin-Didot.fr.Fils & Cie Paris.

CHINESE AND JAPANESE ART.

RUNNING ORNAMENTATION.

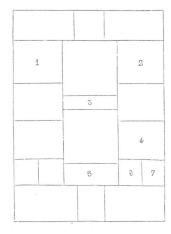

Nos 1, 2, 3, 4, 5, 6, 7.

Come from Chinese sources.

All the others are products of Japanese skill.

It is difficult to produce such powerful effects by means so simple, and Europeans could scarcely do better than study how best to emulate that bold intermixture of intense colours which, directed by Asiatic taste, produces such marvellous results.

FIRMIN-DIDOT FRERES FILS & Cie EDITEURS   Imp. Lemercier & Cie Paris.

INDIAN ART.

ENGRAVINGS IN NIELLO AND ON METALS.

It would be difficult to assign a date to the greater part of the illustrations given in the accompanying plate. This difficulty is nearly always found in dealing with the productions of the extreme East; where the consequence, in an artistic point of view, of the fixity of the religious and political system, is a sort of immobility in perfection, which allows neither progress nor decay. To this cause may also be added that faculty of exact imitation, so characteristic of the Orientals, which enables them to give modern manufactures the appearance of the ancient ones, which are more generally esteemed by amateurs.

However this may be, all must admire the order, propriety, and appreciation of general effect, which distinguish these delicate decorations in metal.

All the specimens given in our plate are taken from objects of daily use.

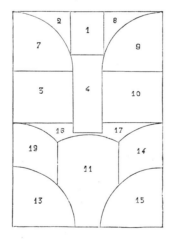

Nᵒˢ 1 to 6.

ORNAMENTS ON TWO NARGHILÉS, belonging to Jacquelet Bey.

Nᵒˢ 7 to 9.

ORNAMENTS ON A EWER, ON THE BOWL OF A EWER, AND ON A PIERCED COVER, belonging to Baroness Rothschild.

Nᵒ 10.

ORNAMENTS ON A EWER, belonging to M. Léonce Mahoù.

Nᵒ 11.

ORNAMENTS ON A DISH, belonging to M. Schefer.

Nᵒˢ 12 to 15.

ORNAMENTS ON A EWER, AND ON DISHES, belonging to M. Verdé-Delisle.

Lith. par Daumont   Imp Lemercier & Cie Paris

INDIAN ART.

PAINTINGS, AND ENGRAVING IN NIELLO.

The various examples, here given, in which appear all the richness and harmony of the Oriental style, have been taken from objects which were shown in the Exhibition organized in 1869, in the Champs-Élysées, by the Central Union of Fine Arts applied to Manufactures. The greater part, it will be observed, serve as decorations of weapons.

Nᵒˢ 1 to 4.

Ornaments taken from a bow belonging to M. Jacquemart.

Nᵒˢ 5 and 6.

Sheath of a dagger, belonging to Col. Bro de Conières.

Nᵒˢ 7 and 8.

Ornaments from the sheath of a sword belonging to M. Jules Michelin.

Nᵒ 9.

Ornament from a weapon belonging to M. Jacquemart.

Nᵒˢ 10 to 12.

Ornaments from the neck of a bottle belonging to M. Reiber.

Nᵒ 13.

Ornaments from a weapon belonging to the Baroness Salomon de Rothschild.

Nᵒ 14.

Rim of a jug, from the same collection.

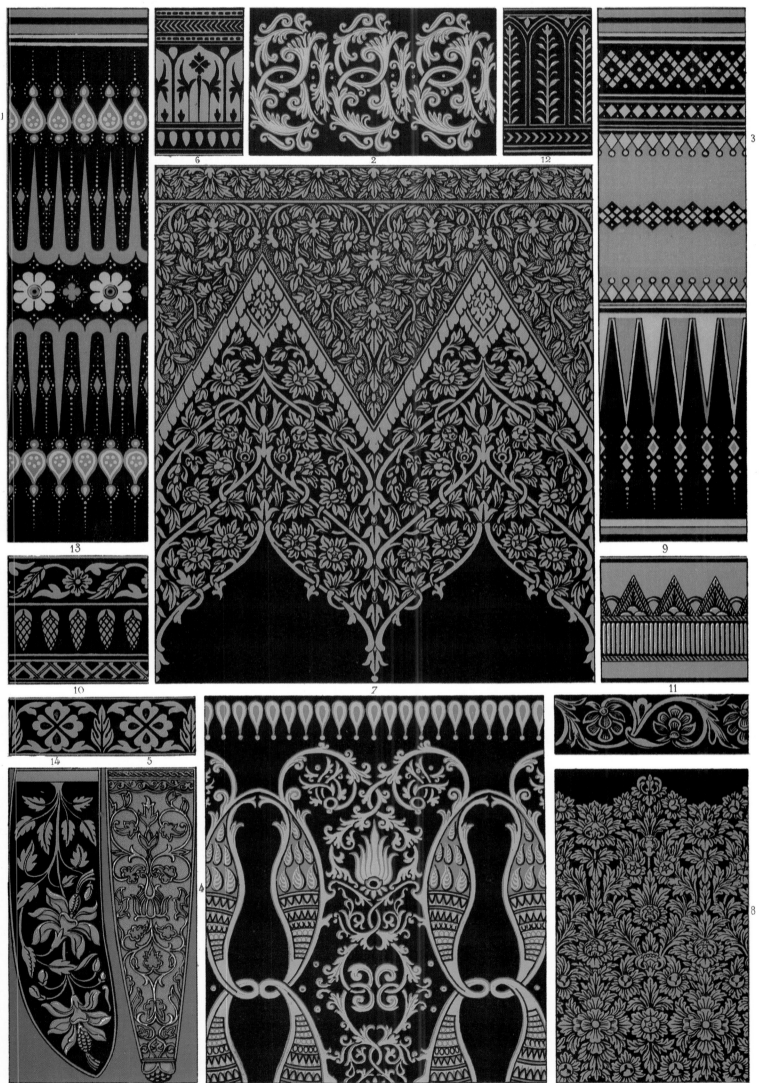

Lith. par Bauer.   Imp.Firmin-Didot fr. Fils &C.ie Paris.

INDIAN ART.

FLORA, AND RUNNING ORNAMENTS,

EMBROIDERY, PAINTING, AND NIELLO.

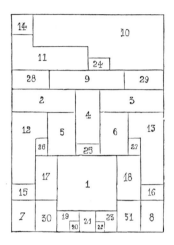

N° 1.

Embroidered fabric, belonging to **M. Moulin.** (*Exposition de l'Union centrale de* 1869.)

N°s 2 to 13.

Borders and grounds from paintings in manuscripts. (Bibl. Nat. *Cabinet des Estampes.*)

N°s 14 to 23.

Borders and grounds from paintings in manuscripts.

N°s 24, 25.

Cloisonnés.

N°s 26, 27.

Embroideries.

N°s 28 to 31.

Engravings in niello from the *Exposition de l'Union centrale de* 1869.

Imp. Firmin-Didot fr. Fils & C.ie Paris.

INDIAN ART.

MODERN DECORATION.

We shall confine ourselves here to a simple enumeration of the subjects in our plate, without referring to the general characteristics of the style.

Nº 1.

A stand of painted wood, belonging to Jacquelet Bey.

Nº 2.

Fragment of an Indian slipper, in velvet, embroidered and spangled, belonging to M. J. Jacquemart.

Nº 3.

Fragment of an Indian slipper, embroidered in gold and mother of pearl on a velvet ground, belonging to M. J. Jacquemart.

Nᵒˢ 4, 5.

Subjects taken from a dagger, onyx ground with gold enamel, belonging to the Baroness Salomon de Rothschild.

Nᵒˢ 6, 7.

Goblet on a small pedestal, belonging to the same.

Nᵒˢ 8, 9.

Borders of miniatures; Bibl. Nat.

Nᵒˢ 10, 11.

Palm-leaves, from miniatures; Bibl. Nat.

Nº 12.

Tray, papier-mâché, belonging to M. Bellenot.

Nᵒˢ 13, 14, 15.

Goblets of the same material, belonging to the same.

Nᵒˢ 16 to 19.

Ornaments on papier-mâché objects, belonging to M. Verdé-Delisle.

Except Nᵒˢ 8, 9, 10, 11, all these objects were exhibited in the *Exposition de l'Union centrale des arts appliqués à l'Industrie*, 1869.

Lith. par F. Durin.

Imp. Firmin-Didot Fr. Fils & Cie Paris

PERSIAN ART

PRINTED LINEN.

FIGURES OF FLOWERS AND ANIMALS.

It is unnecessary to remind our readers of the popularity which chintzes have so long enjoyed, and of the part they still take in the ordinary furniture of houses. It was especially during the last century that the French manufactories for the imitation of these fabrics carried on so extensive a trade; but they are still so much in use that it cannot be superfluous to give examples of some of the best original models, in order to preserve the style, and prevent too great a deviation from it.

In the examples given in our plate — fabrics of Eastern manufacture, in which the Persian style properly so called seems in some points to resemble the Indian — we shall find in addition to the Persian flora, figures of animals (especially birds), and even the human figure (1), treated in a manner which keeps a middle course between the imitation of nature and the employment of conventional forms, sometimes inserted arbitrarily and without reference to surrounding objects, and at others grouped in the form of a regular ornament, as in the fragment to the left of the plate, at the lower corner.

(1) Notwithstanding the somewhat singular appearance of the figure in the centre of the composition we have thought it better not to modify it in any way, as to do so would have caused a want of accuracy and have taken from the object the certificate of its origin.

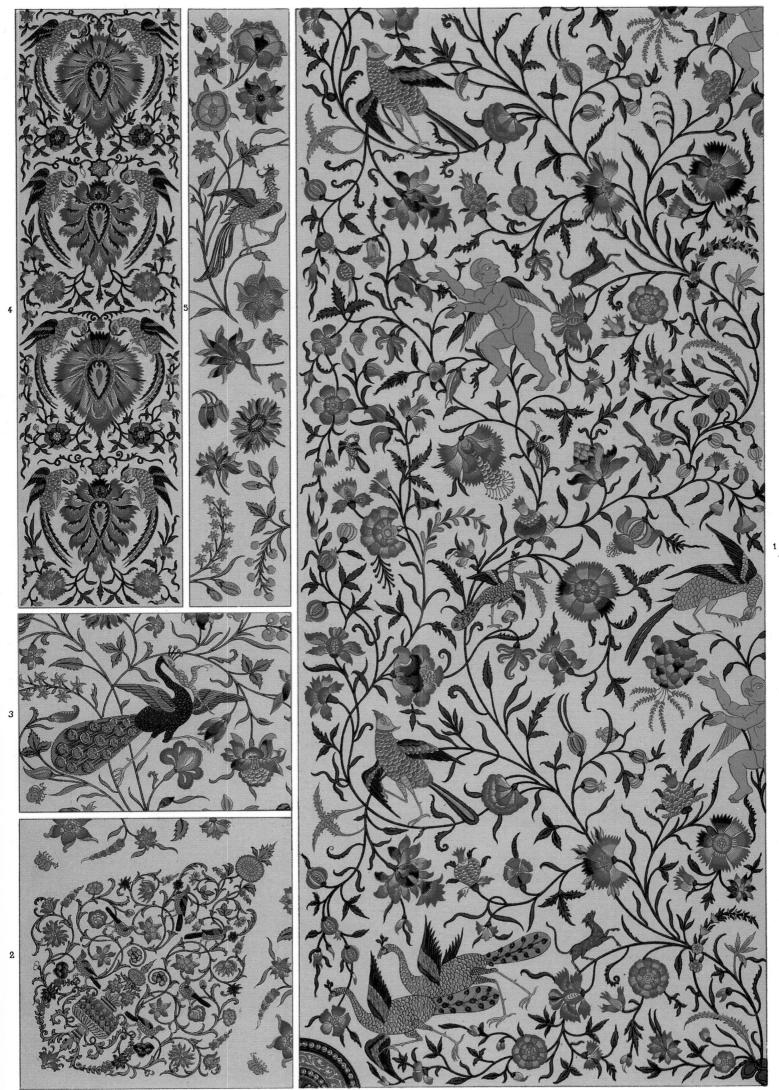

Lithographie par F. Durin   Imp. Firmin-Didot fr. Fils & Cie Paris

PERSIAN ART.

ENGRAVINGS IN NIELLO.

The black grounds of these ornaments are obtained by crossed lines filled in with black as may be seen in Nº 1.

The black of these grounds is therefore not absolute, as in the reduced scale of the plate it has necessarily been made to appear; hence the original has a still richer and more harmonious effect.

13		7		10	
11				12	
14	5	15	6	14 bis	
1		3		2	
5		9		4	

Nº 1.

Design taken from a bowl. (Comte de Mornay.)

Nº 2.

Design taken from a bowl. (M. Schefer.)

Nᵒˢ 3, 4.

Angular patterns from the necks of vases. (M. Méchin.)

Nᵒˢ 5, 6.

Running designs (M. Schefer.)

Nᵒˢ 7, 8.

Borders taken from a bowl. (M. Reiber.)

Nᵒˢ 9, 10.

Borders taken from a bowl. (M. Goupil.)

Nº 11.

Borders from a bowl. (Comte de Mornay.)

Nº 12.

Borders from a bowl. (M. Dick.)

Nº 13.

Borders from a snuff-box. (M. Collinot.)

Nᵒˢ 14, 14 bis, (in conjunction).

Borders from a vase. (M. Schefer.)

Nº 15.

Cartouche from a bowl. (M. Crampon.)

All these objects were exhibited in the *Exposition de l'Union centrale des arts industriels,* 1869.

Lith. par Laugier   Imp. Firmin-Didot fr. Fils & Cie, Paris.

PERSIAN ART.

EARTHENWARE.

The various examples in our plate give an accurate idea of the patterns commonly employed in Persian earthenware.

These patterns usually consist of pure arabesques, frequently combined with ornamental flowers, the drawing of which more or less resembles natural types. Among them it is easy to recognize the rose, the Indian pink, the tulip, the hyacinth, etc.... Sometimes too, the subject is animated by some chimerical figure, such as the bird occupying the centre of the magnificent dish belonging to the Comte de Nieuwerkerke.

The following are the sources from whence we have taken our examples.

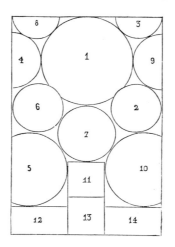

DISHES.

N° 1.

Collection of the Comte de Nieuwerkerke, Superintendent of Museums.

N°ˢ to 5.

Collection of M. Scheffer.

N°ˢ 6, 7.

Collection of Dʳ Mandl.

N° 8.

Collection of M. Lequen.

N° 9.

Collection of M. P. Saline.

N° 10.

Collection of Baron de Seneval.

GLAZED TILES.

N°ˢ 11, 12.

Collection of M. Parvillée.

N° 13.

Collection of Dʳ Meymar.

N° 14.

Collection of M. Collinot.

All the above objects were shown in the Oriental Exhibition of 1869, organized by the Central Union of Fine Arts applied to Manufactures.

Lith. par Lebreton et Bailly   Imp. Firmin-Didot, fr. Fils & C.ie Paris

PERSIAN ART.

_____

TAPESTRY, AND RUNNING ORNAMENTS.

The carpet represented in the accompanying plate belongs to the finest period of Persian art, the sixteenth century of our era. The natural flower, in such frequent use amongst the Persians, takes quite a secondary part therein while the conventional flora appears in all its splendour. This carpet contains the most important varieties of the Oriental palm; the arrangement of the colours is extremely good and quite typical. It belongs to M. Bouvier, painter.

The nine specimens of running ornament come from two copies of the *Schah Nameh*, a work to which we have already referred (plate 🏺), belonging to the Bibl. Nat. (489 and 494, *Réserve, supplément persan*). They contain very interesting elementary geometrical designs, although in the use of this kind of ornament the Persians have not, on the whole, equalled the Arabs or the Moors.

Lith. par Le Breton.

Imp. Firmin-Didot fr Fils & Cie Paris.

PERSIAN ART.

DECORATIONS OF MANUSCRIPTS.

The first of the two subjects composing the accompanying plate represents a page from the *Châh Namèh* or *Schah-Nameh,* a manuscript in the National Library, Paris (Persian Supplement, N° 489, Reserve); the second a page from another copy of the same work also in manuscript and belonging to the same library (Supplement N° 494).

The *Schah-Nameh* is a history in verse of the ancient Kings of Persia by Abul Casim Mansur Firdusi, who spent thirty years in the composition of the poem, which consists of 60,000 distiches, and is dedicated to the celebrated Mahmud the Ghaznevide. Firdusi died in the year 411 of the Hegira (1020 of our era).

This poem, which is one of the most important works in the Persian language, has been the subject of numerous philological studies. A very fine edition has lately been published at the *Imprimerie Nationale,* the translation of which, and the notes, as well as the revision of the text, are due to M. J. Mohl, of the Institute of France.

The manuscript N° 489 was bought at Ispahan by Otter, and appears to have come from the library of the Sofis.

The National Library also possesses another copy of *Schah-Nameh,* of very great beauty, bearing the date 1012 of the Hegira, and entered in the Persian Supplement, under N° 490 of the Reserve.

Lithographie par Picard.

Imp. Firmin-Didot fr. Fils & Cie, Paris.

PERSIAN ART.

CARPETS.

The accompanying plate shows the ground and border of a kneeling-carpet of Persian manufacture, in which the boldness and elegance of the scrolls are as remarkable as the perfect harmony of the colours.

The cloth ground is ornamented with raised embroidery of the same material edged with silk (1).

The peculiar form of the flowers on the white and black grounds, and also on the corners of the black ground of the principal subject, shows the influence that Indian and Persian art have exercised on each other, and also the closeness of their resemblance.

(1) This beautiful carpet excited much attention in the exhibition of the *Union centrale des Beaux-Arts appliqués à l'industrie*, where it formed a part of the Oriental Museum. It is to the kindness of M. Léonce Mahoû, to whom it belongs, that we are indebted for its reproduction here.

Lith par F Durin

Imp Firmin-Didot fr Fils & Cie, Paris

PL. XXV.

ARABIAN ART.

BINDING.

This plate represents the binding of the large Koran belonging to M. Ambroise Firmin Didot, roses and borders from which fill the two succeeding plates.

This Koran is of very large dimensions, measuring no less than 3 ft. 5 inches in length and 1 ft. 8 $\frac{1}{2}$ inches in breadth.

Although the manuscript ornamentation of the pages reproduced in the succeeding plates presents a mixture of the Persian and Arabian styles, in the binding pure Arabian art, characterized by strict adherence to geometrical forms, is alone visible.

The principal effect is produced by combinations of roses, in the use and arrangement of which the Arabs have at all times displayed so much taste and ingenuity. In this class of composition interest attaches mainly to the incidental figure which arises from the meeting of two roses of unequal size. This incidental figure is worthy of interest in the present example, for the geometric clasp is in itself valuable, its wide double heptagon destroying the monotony that might otherwise be found in the style. The design in the centre of the lower part of the plate is a border from a corner of the same binding.

The other borders are taken from the interior and exterior edges.

Dufour & Bauer, lith.

Imp Firmin-Didot fr Fils & Cie Paris.

ARABIAN ART.

ILLUMINATIONS OF MANUSCRIPTS.

ROSE-WORK.

The roses grouped in the accompanying plate are all taken from a richly adorned manuscript of the Koran, of unusual size, which, at the present time, forms part of the library of M. Ambroise Firmin Didot.

Arabian art is well represented in it, not merely by the complete absence of living figures, the representation of which was forbidden by the Koran, but also by the excellence of the geometrical combinations. Several of the characteristics mentioned by Owen Jones (*Grammar of Ornament*), as typical of Arabian decoration, are to be found in it; such, for example, as the continual interlacing of curved lines attached to a common centre and radiating towards the circumference. This is especially to be noticed in the rose in the centre of the plate.

The use of the flower combined with the lineal ornament of which it forms a part shows in some degree the influence of Persian Art upon Arabian ornamentation.

Lith par F. Durin.

Imp. Firmin-Didot fr. Fils & Cie, Paris.

ARABIAN ART.

ILLUMINATIONS OF MANUSCRIPTS.

ORNAMENTED INSCRIPTIONS.

The fragments of which this plate is composed, have been taken from the same sources as those of the rose-work, pl. ⚖. They are from the large illuminated Koran which forms a part of the library of M. Ambroise Firmin Didot. What we there said of the general style of these paintings, is also applicable here.

The subjects represented are taken from the borders of the ornamented inscriptions in Cufic (old Arabic) characters which separate the hundred and fourteen principal divisions of the text. There are examples of these characters in the two fragments on each side of the central rose.

The nature of these ornaments renders them essentially suitable as models of great variety and beauty in the art of gold and silver enamelling.

The influence of Persian art in this style of decoration has already been shown, and here we find traces, as easily recognised, of the Byzantine style. See for instance the angle that occupies the left, in the lower part of the plate.

Lith par Dufour & F Durin.   Imp.Firmin-Didot fr.& Fils & Cie Paris

MOORISH ART.

MOSAICS, AND ENAMELLED TERRA-COTTA.

All the specimens in this plate come from the Alhambra and from the Alcazar of Seville.

Most of them are examples of the Arab style in all its geometrical purity; a few however, in which the floral ornament appears, belong rather to the Hispano-Moorish style.

The separate tiles are of great interest to modern industry, not only for their unique type, but also for the rich designs in endless variety into which they may be arranged.

Dufour et Sanier lith.

Imp. Firmin Didot fr. Fils & Cie Paris

MOORISH ART.

ARCHITECTURAL DECORATION.

The various specimens collected in the accompanying plate are all taken from the Alhambra, that marvellous palace of the Moorish kings of Granada, and the most complete expression of the style which borrowed its first elements from the Byzantines, while developing them with greater richness and amplitude. What is most striking in this system (and it is a merit of the first order in architectural decoration) is, that the grand features of the ornamentation are in accordance with the true principles of building, which unite with them in harmonizing the details.

It is for this reason that notwithstanding their low superadded reliefs, these ornaments appear, by an agreeable illusion, to add to the solidity of the building they decorate.

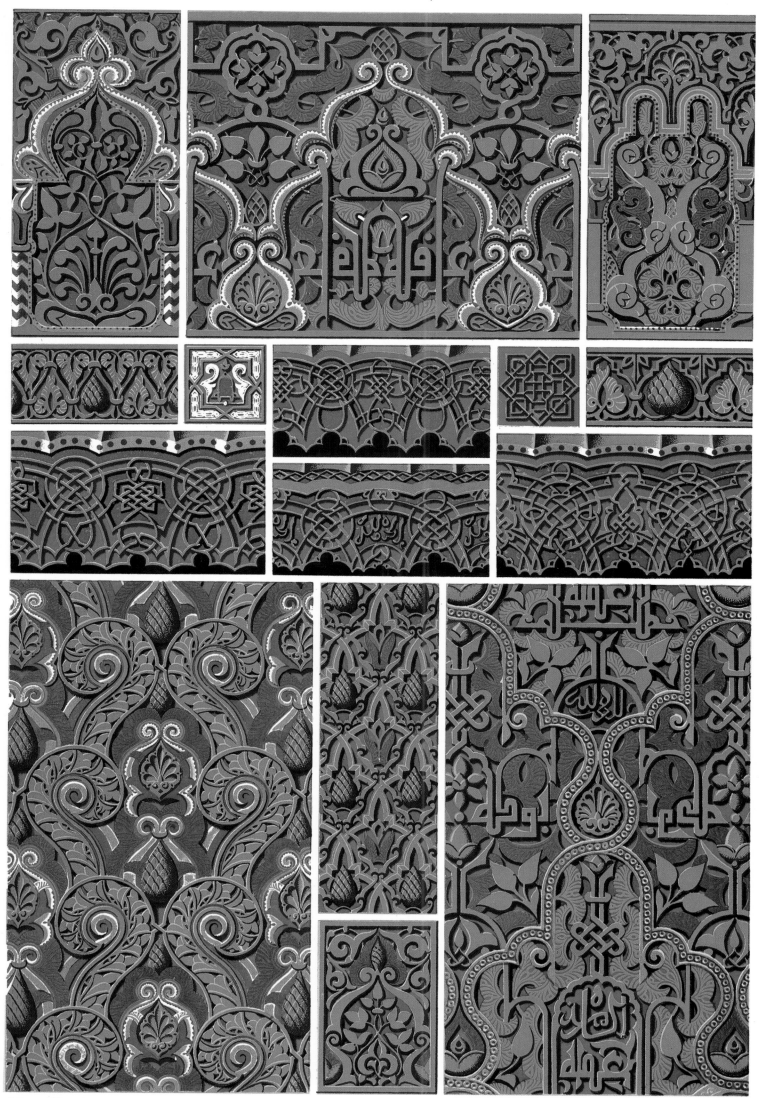

Lith par F Durin

Imp. Firmin-Didot fr. Fils & Cie, Paris

BYZANTINE ART.

MURAL PAINTINGS, MOSAICS,

AND

PAINTINGS FROM MANUSCRIPTS.

We class the subjects in the accompanying plate in historical order, commencing with the earliest.

Nos 1 to 5.

Paintings in St Sophia, dating from the sixth century, after Salzenberg.

These paintings are almost exactly in the Greek style.

MOSAICS.

No 6.

Church of St George at Thessalonica, after C. Texier. (*L'Arménie, la Perse et la Mésopotamie*, 2 vols. folio, Firmin Didot.)

Nos 7 to 16.

Paintings collected at Constantinople, seventh and eighth centuries, after Salzenberg.

No 17.

Enamelled border.

Nos 18 to 28.

Marginal paintings, eighth and ninth centuries, ancient ornaments little altered. (Bibl. Nat., Réserve. MS. 139; Greek section.)

Nos 29, 30.

Paintings from a manuscript executed about 860 for the Emperor Basil the Macedonian. (Bibl. Nat., Réserve, No 510, Greek section.)

Nos 31, 32.

Manuscript. (Bibl. Nat., Réserve, No 64; Greek section.)

Nos 33, 34.

Mosaics; the first from Palermo, the second from Monreale, twelfth century.

Nos 35 to 40.

Details from the various manuscripts mentioned above.

MIDDLE AGES.

VIII CENTURY.

DECORATIONS OF MANUSCRIPTS.

The thirty-eight examples given in our plate belong to a transition period of great interest, the interval between the Greco-Roman or Pompeian style (the traces of which are specially noticeable in Nᵒˢ 2, 3, 5, 7, 10, 11, 13, 18, 29, 30, 32), and the Byzantine style properly so called. All are taken from illuminations of manuscripts, in which ornamental art seems to have sought refuge during a considerable part of the middle ages. They are copied from the following manuscripts.

<table>
<tr><td style="text-align:center">Nᵒˢ 1 to 26.
GOSPELS OF SAINT-SERNIN (Toulouse).
Latin manuscript written by Godescald for the Emperor Charlemagne.
Library of the Louvre.</td><td style="text-align:center">Nᵒˢ 27 to 38.
GOSPELS OF SAINT-MÉDARD (Soissons).
Latin manuscript.
Bibliothèque Nationale.</td></tr>
</table>

If any of our readers should wish to study this interesting style more fully, we refer them to the work of Comte Aug. de Bastard, *Peintures et ornements des manuscrits.* (Paris, 1835; impl. folio.)

MIDDLE AGES.

BYZANTINE STYLE.

MOSAIC, INLAID-WORK, ENGRAVING IN NIELLO, AND PAINTING.

The following is a plan of the contents of the plate, with details of the sources whence the examples have been obtained.

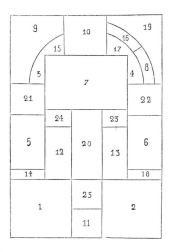

Nᵒˢ 1 to 4.

The churches of St. George, St. Demetrius, and St. Sophia at Thessalonica. (From M. C. Texier : *Description de l'Asie Mineure*, 3 vols. folio, *Firmin Didot*.)

Nᵒˢ 5, 6.

CATHEDRAL of Ravello.

Nᵒˢ 7, 8.

CATHEDRAL of Monreale.

Nᵒˢ 9, 10.

ZIZA CHAPEL, at Palermo.

Nᵒ 11.

PALATINE CHAPEL, at Palermo.

Nᵒˢ 12 to 17.

GREEK MANUSCRIPT, Bibliothèque Nationale, Nᵒ 64.

Nᵒ 18.

Another Greek MS. Nᵒ 139.

Nᵒ 19.

Another Greek MS. Nᵒ 230.

Nᵒˢ 20 to 22.

TAKEN from the *Memorie spettanti alla Calcografia del comm. Conte Leopoldo Cicognara*, 1831.

We are indebted to M. Moyaux, architect, for the mosaics from Palermo, copied by him from the originals, as well as for the other objects from the same source which figure in plate .

Lith. par F. Durin.

Imp. Firmin-Didot fr Fils & Cᵗᵉ Paris.

MIDDLE AGES.

BYZANTINE ORNAMENTS.

These ornaments, which are interesting both from an historical and artistic point of view, are all — with the exception of the flower occupying the centre of the upper part of the plate — taken from a very curious manuscript in the *Bibliothèque nationale* (Latin supplement, Nº 1075), entitled *Évangéliaire ou Apocalypse d'Aquitaine ou d'Espagne.*

The central flower is taken from another Greek manuscript in the same library (B. N. Réserve, Nº 230.)

Independently of the original value of these fragments obtained from a source which is very little known, it is interesting to notice, from the examples they offer, the very manifest influence of Byzantine on Arabian art — a phenomenon which is not rare in the history of nations, where we frequently find the conquering power borrowing and adapting to itself the arts of the conquered.

It is especially in the red and yellow leaves on the pink ground in Nº 1, and also in Nᵒˢ 5, 6, 7, 8, 9, and 13 to 17, that we find the outlines and general forms appropriated by Arabian art, though with greater breadth and simplicity, and in compositions of greater power.

Lith par Pralon

Imp. Firmin-Didot fr. & Fils & Cⁱᵉ, Paris

BYZANTINE ART.

MOSAICS, FILIGREE ENAMELS, AND EMBROIDERIES.

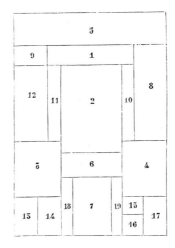

Numbers 1 to 7 represent mosaics in the Ziza chapel at Palermo. The drawings were taken by M. Hittorff, by whose son they have been kindly communicated to us.

Numbers 8 to 11 represent *cloisonné* and filigree enamels, designed as settings for precious stones, after a copy of the Gospels in the Louvre.

The specimens numbered 12 to 19 are taken from frescoes in a monastery near Trebizonde, collected by M. Charles Texier. They represent fragments of the embroidered materials, ornamented with pearls and precious stones, with which the Byzantines clothed themselves from head to foot. It was this wide-spread taste for objects of costly workmanship, that caused St. Chrysostom to say : « All our admiration is now reserved for goldsmiths and weavers. »

« Artists, » says Batissier, « were obliged to renounce their old traditions, in order to create new types, and they strove rather for richness of effect, than for beauty. »

MARCVS

ΘCCEMA TER

BEATRIX MEINHONORE DEI O

Durin lith

Imp.Firmin-Didot.fr.Fils & Cie Paris.

MIDDLE AGES.

XII CENTURY.

DECORATIONS IN MOSAIC.

The sixteen specimens of mosaic work grouped in our plate are obtained from the following sources.

N°s 1 to 12.

PALATINE CHAPEL AT PALERMO.

The probable date and style of this edifice are thus described by Batissier (*Histoire de l'art monumental dans l'antiquité et au moyen-âge,* p. 397) :

« When the Normans arrived in Sicily, that province was rich in monuments. King Roger could not help admiring them extremely, and in the buildings undertaken by him he employed Byzantine architects, who had already adopted the innovations made in architecture by Arabian taste. The churches built by the new conquerors present an evident combination of the Greek and Latin styles.

« Amongst the most beautiful and curious basilicas of that century that have come down to us, is the Chapel Royal of Palermo, built about the year 1129, by King Roger, all the arcades of which are pointed, and the ceiling divided into compartments. »

N°s 13, 14, 15.

PALACE OF THE ZISA, AT PALERMO.

N° 16.

CATHEDRAL OF SALERNO.

MOYEN ÂGE

Lithographié par G. Sanier.

Imp. Firmin-Didot fr. Fils & Cie Paris

MIDDLE AGES.

XIV AND XV CENTURIES.

MARQUETRY.

The first twenty numbers in the accompanying plate represent mosaics in ivory and wood on the Poissy altar-screen, a magnificent work in ivory, in the finest style of the fourteenth century, and so much admired in the Louvre.

This altar-screen was presented in 1416, by John of France, brother of Charles V, and by Jeanne, Countess of Auvergne and Boulogne, his second wife, whom he had married in 1389.

N⁰ˢ 21 to 27 are taken from various ivory boxes of the same period in the Sauvageot collection.

N⁰ˢ 28 to 31 represent mosaics in wood of the fifteenth century taken from the pulpit of Saint Ambrose at Milan.

These various examples, although many of them belong to a period more or less approaching the Renaissance, are in the Byzantine style. An art like marquetry, which can only be worked by simple means, is little likely to follow the successive modifications of decorative art.

Lith. par Daumont.

Imp. Firmin Didot fr. Fils &C.ᵉ Paris

MIDDLE AGES.

VII, VIII AND IX CENTURIES.

CELTIC ORNAMENTS.

Celtic is the name most frequently given to this style by those who have studied it most recently; it is, however, often called *Anglo-Saxon*. Some critics consider it to be a mixture of the Scandinavian and Byzantine styles, but it is considered by others, especially by J. O. Westwood, (See *The Grammar of Ornament* by Owen Jones,) as indigenous and due entirely to the primitive inhabitants of the British Isles. As essential characteristics of this style in its earliest period, the same writer mentions : 1st the absence of all imitations of foliage or plants; 2ndly the exclusive use of simple geometrical figures, interlacings of ribbons, diagonal or spiral lines, etc.

It is to this style that the thirty-three examples given in the accompanying plate refer. They are taken from the following documents :

VII CENTURY.

Nos 1, 3, 5, 6, 7, 9, 11, 12, 13, 25, 28, 29, 30.

THE GOSPELS, OR BOOK OF DURROW. (Trinity College, Dublin.)
Symbols of the Evangelists and ornamental pages.

Nos 4, 33.

Frontispiece of the Gospels of Saint Mark and Saint Luke.

No 26.

THE LINDISFARNE GOSPELS.
Ornamental page.

Nos 22, 31.

THE GOSPELS OF SAINT LUKE. (British Museum.)
Frontispiece.

VIII CENTURY.

No 18.

COMMENTARIES ON THE PSALMS BY CASSIODORUS « *manu Bedæ* ».
(Library of Durham Cathedral.)
David conquering.

Nos 8, 24.

The Royal Psalmist.

Nos 2, 14.

THE GOSPEL OF SAINT MATTHEW, WITH THE SYMBOLS OF THE EVANGELISTS.
(Library of the Convent of Saint-Gall.)

IX CENTURY.

No 6.

LATIN GOSPEL. (Library of Saint-Gall.)
Ornamental page, and the Transfiguration.

No 10.

MANUSCRIPT IN THE SAME LIBRARY.
The Crucifixion.

No 27.

PSALTER AT St JOHN'S BOLL., CAMBRIDGE.
Victory of David over Goliath, and over the Lion, and commencement of Psalms 1 and 102.

The other, and less important subjects (Nos 15, 16, 17, 19, 20, 21, 23, 32) are taken from Manuscripts in the Bodleian Library at Oxford, the Library of the Convent of Saint-Gall, and the Library of Trinity College, Dublin.

As regards the specimens the names of which have been given above, it may be noted, that the subjects of which they form a part are given in full by J. O. Westwood in his great work, *Fac-Similes of the Miniatures and Ornaments of Anglo-Saxon and Irish Manuscripts,* to which we must refer those who desire to make a thorough study of this particular branch of art, as, in accordance with our plan we are limited to giving only some of the most striking examples, such as those comprised in our plate.

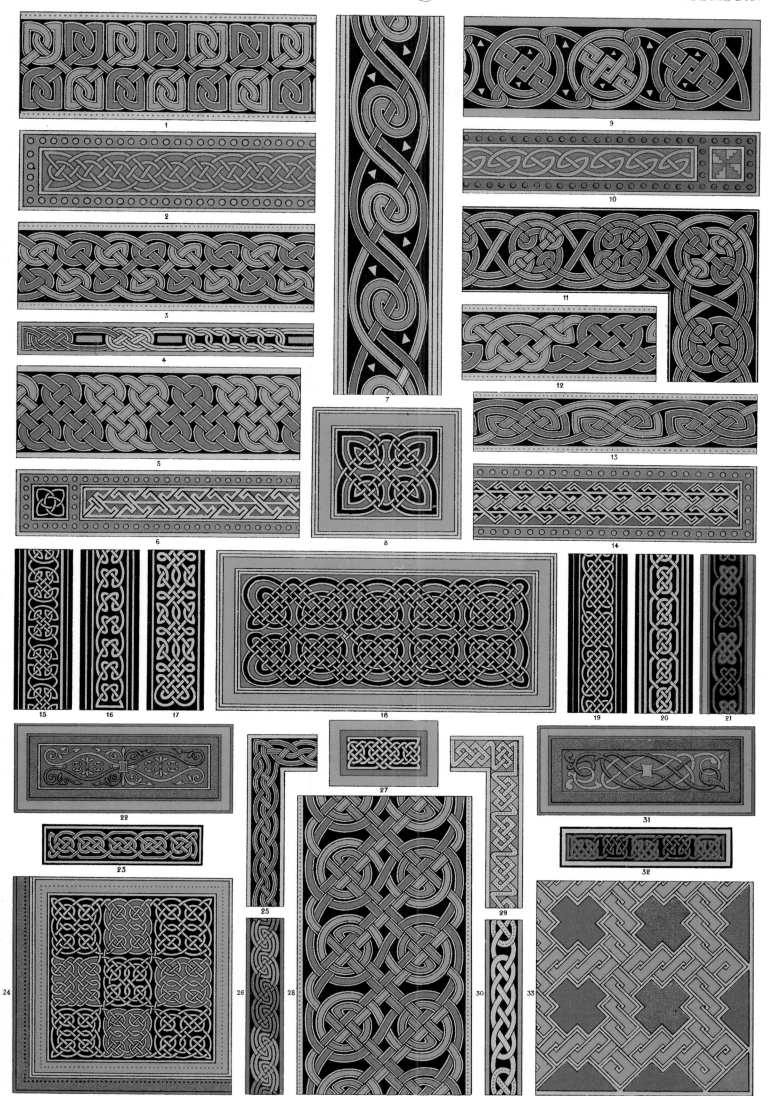

Lithographié par Painlevé.

Imp. Firmin-Didot fr. Fils & Cie. Paris.

MIDDLE AGES.

VII, VIII, IX, X AND XI CENTURIES.

CELTIC ORNAMENTS.

We have already explained the origin of this name, given by modern criticism to the productions of Northern art during a certain portion of the Middle Ages.

The plate to which we allude presented this style in its first phase, characterized by the exclusive use of purely lineal and geometrical combinations; and the most ancient of the documents collected in this plate belong to the same style (N°s 1 to 12).

But this style begins to change in N°s 13, 15, and 16 (eighth and ninth centuries), and we see the heads of chimerical animals appearing in the midst of interlacings, which they terminate; and afterwards the further we advance into the ninth and tenth centuries, the more does the line lose its mathematical regularity, and the more free does the form become, assuming at last all the varieties and caprices of nature. It is to this period, called the time of *exfoliation*, that N°s 18 to 33 (tenth and eleventh centuries) belong. Lastly, in the four magnificent initial letters bearing the numbers 34 to 37, we find perfectly united those two elements of fancy and symmetry, which should never be separated in well arranged decorations.

The 36 subjects in the plate may be thus grouped.

7th CENTURY.

N°s 1 to 6.

THE GOSPELS OF DURROW. (Trin. Coll., Dublin.

N°s 7 and 8.

BOOK OF KELLS. (Trin. Coll., Dublin.)

N°s 9 and 10.

ROYAL Manuscripts M. S. I. E, VI. (British Museum.)

7th AND 8th CENTURIES.

N° 11.

CODEX AUREUS. (Royal Library, Stockholm.

8th CENTURY.

N° 12.

GOSPELS OF THOMAS, Abbot of Hohenaugia. (Library of Trèves.)

N° 13.

COMMENTARIES ON THE PSALMS, by Cassiodorus. (Library of Durham Cathedral.)

8th AND 9th CENTURIES.

N° 14.

GOSPELS OF St CHAD. (Lichfield Cathedral.)

9th CENTURY.

N° 15.

PSALTER. (St John's Coll., Cambridge.)

N°s 16, 17.

GOSPELS OF MAC DURNAN. (Archiepiscopal Library, Lambeth.)

10th CENTURY.

N° 18.

LATIN GOSPELS. (Trin. Coll., Cambridge.)

N°s 19 to 21.

CODEX VOSSIANUS. (Bodleian Library.)

N° 22.

BENEDICTIONALE OF St ETHELWULF. (Duke of Devonshire's Library.)

11th CENTURY.

N°s 23 and 24.

GRAND LATIN PSALTER. (Public Library at Boulogne.)

N°s 25 to 33.

ARUNDEL PSALTER. (British Museum.)

N°s 34 to 37.

INITIAL LETTERS FROM THE ABBEY OF St GERMAIN DES PRÉS. (Library of M. Ambroise Firmin Didot.)

. par Bauer

Imp. Firmin-Didot fr Fils & C.ᵉ Paris

MIDDLE AGES.

XI AND XII CENTURIES.

ROMANESQUE STYLE.

PAINTINGS.

The specimens in this plate are taken from two important manuscripts, both belonging to M. Ambroise Firmin Didot.

The first is a folio commentary of Beatus on the Apocalypse, a manuscript of the twelfth century, which reproduces on a larger scale the greater part of the paintings of another manuscript which may have belonged to the eighth.

The second is a folio copy of the Gospels, the rich decorations of which furnish most varied examples of the architecture and painting of the eleventh and twelfth centuries. It was written at the commencement of the twelfth century for the use of the Abbey of Luxeuil in Franche-Comté, a branch of the celebrated Abbey of Saint Colomban.

Gérard, abbot of Luxeuil, speaks of himself as its author : *auctor codicis hujus,* and names himself elsewhere, alluding to the situation of his abbey :

> *Luxovii pastor Gerardus lucis amator,*
> *Dando Petro hunc librum, lumen mihi posco supernum.*

In front of each of the Gospels there is a page coloured in purple or blue, and decorated in the style of the silks of that period, representing fantastic animals, and apparently belonging to a period anterior to the paintings of the manuscript. It was the custom then to enclose each Gospel in silk or vellum ornamented with miniatures in the style of tapestries.

The character of the ornaments is Romanesque, that is to say of both Latin and Greek origin, otherwise called Byzantine. The amplitude of the deeply indented foliage and the mixture of natural and fantastic figures all bear witness to the last of transformation of antique ornament, properly so called, still employed in architecture in the decoration of the semi-circle. It was scarcely before the thirteenth century that the imitation of indigenous flora, trefoils, quatre-foils and volute of crossettes changed the aspect of decoration to that style which is called Gothic or pointed.

In the accompanying plan given below, N°s 1 to 16 belong to the manuscript of Beatus, the others to the manuscript of Luxeuil.

MOYEN ÂGE

Lith par Daumont

Imp. Firmin-Didot fr. Fils & Cie Paris.

MIDDLE AGES.

EMBROIDERIES, PAINTINGS, AND ENAMELS.

The specimens contained in this plate may be classified in the following way, according to the sources from which they are derived.

11		4	12
5			6
9		1	10
7			8
28		3	29
16		13	18
17		14	19
		15	
20			24
21		2	25
22			26
23			27

Nᵒˢ 1 to 4.

Fabrics of silk and gold of the twelfth century, found in the tombs of the abbaye Saint-Germain des Prés. (A. Lenoir, *Statistique monumentale de Paris.*)

Nᵒˢ 5 to 8.

Mural paintings of the thirteenth century from the chapel of Notre-Dame de la Roche (Seine-et-Oise), and from the Jacobin convent at Agen.

Nᵒˢ 9 to 15.

Mural paintings from the churches of Amencharads-Rada and Edshult, in Sweden, from the fine work of M. M. Mandelgren.

Nᵒˢ 16 to 27.

Enamels from the great reliquary in the treasury of Aix-la-Chapelle.

Nᵒˢ 28, 29.

Fragments of miniatures.

Durin lith.

Imp.Firmin-Didot fr. Fils & Cie. Paris

MIDDLE AGES.

XIV CENTURY.

ILLUMINATIONS OF MANUSCRIPTS.

The various designs of which this plate is composed are all taken from a remarkable manuscript belonging to the *Bibliothèque nationale* (*Book of St. Thomas Aquinas*, in Latin, folio, N° 7241⁵; Codex Colbert, 1301).

These interesting illuminations must be referred to Italian art of the fourteenth century. They are in remarkable conformity with those of the manuscript of the *Statuts de l'ordre du Saint-Esprit au droit désir ou du nœud*, of which count Horace de Vielcastel, in the preface to his reproduction of the same (Engelmann and Graff, 1853), says :

« The date of 1352, which it bears, brings its pictures into the schools of Cimabue and Giotto (the former of whom was still living in 1302,
« and the latter died in 1336); and, indeed, the style of these beautiful miniatures bears the character of the school of these celebrated artists,
« especially that of Simone Memmi. »

These ornaments, which for their precision and boldness are as applicable to metal work, especially in iron, as to the decoration of flat surfaces, occupy an important place in the art which serves as a sort of transition between the Byzantine style modified by Moorish art, and that of the Renaissance.

Imp. Firmin-Didot fr. Fils & Cie, Paris.

MIDDLE AGES.

PAINTINGS ON MANUSCRIPTS.

The sixteen unnumbered examples in our plate have been taken from an Italian manuscript of the fourteenth century, attributed to Simone Memmi, of whom we have already spoken in plate.  They form a continuation of the examples contained in that plate, the principal characteristics being the same in both, though in the accompanying illustration there is greater variety in the shapes, and a more frequent use of the human figure and of the forms of animals.

N°s 17, 18, 19 and 20, are also Italian, and may be regarded as types of the marginal decorations and initial letters of the manuscripts of the fifteenth century. They are taken from a Suetonius and a Justinian lent by M. Bachelin-Deflorenne.

Lith par Daumont   Imp.Firmin-Didot fr. Fils & Cie Paris.

MIDDLE AGES.

XII, XIII AND XIV CENTURIES.

STAINED GLASS.

The want of space between the different subjects collected in this illustration does not allow us to indicate the numbers on the plate itself, so we give a small sketch below, with the corresponding numbers.

Nos 1 to 5. CATHEDRAL OF CHARTRES.		Nos 24 to 26. CATHEDRAL OF LYONS.
Nos 6 to 12. CATHEDRAL OF BOURGES.		Nos 27 to 29. CATHEDRAL OF ANGERS.
Nos 13 to 15. CATHEDRAL OF COLOGNE.		Nos 30 to 33. CHURCH OF SAINT URBAN AT TROYES.
No 16. CHURCH OF SAINT CUNIBERT, COLOGNE.		Nos 34, 35. CATHEDRAL OF STRASBOURG.
Nos 17, 18. CATHEDRAL OF SOISSONS.		Nos 36 to 38. CATHEDRAL OF ROUEN.
Nos 19 to 23. CATHEDRAL OF LE MANS.		No 39. CATHEDRAL OF SENS.

It is, as may easily be seen, from the best times of church window ornamentation that our examples have been taken, for, though it is impossible to render anything like their brilliancy and transparency, yet it is well to bring before the public designs and combinations of colours as models for an industry still in full activity.

The specimens chosen present, for the most part, general forms, which might be utilized in many different combinations.

Our readers may refer to the work of the Abbés Cahier and Martin (*Monographie des vitraux de la cathédrale de Bourges; Paris, Poussielgue-Rusand*, 1844), if they wish to know more of this interesting period of French national art — a period of which an eminent critic has said : « Painting on enamel and glass, sculpture and working in gold were sufficiently advanced to harmonize worthily with architectural science, which had recently expanded and drawn an inspiration from the magical aspects of Oriental buildings. » (*Origine et progrès de l'art, études et recherches*, par P. A. Jeanron; 1849.)

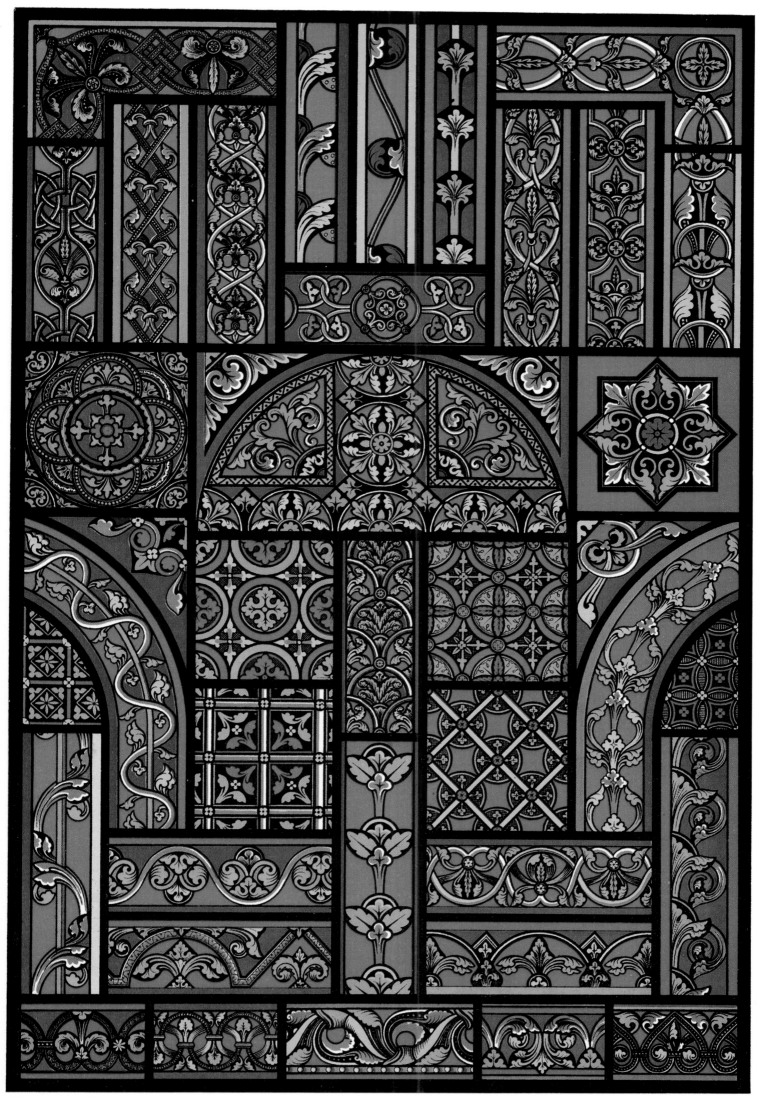

Lith. par Dufour et Lebreton

Imp. Firmin-Didot fr. Fils & Cᵉ Paris.

MIDDLE AGES.

XIII, XIV, AND XV CENTURIES.

GRISAILLE WINDOWS.

Nᵒˢ 1 to 23.

Cologne Cathedral.

Nᵒˢ 24 to 27.

Borders selected from the monograph of Bourges Cathedral.

Nᵒˢ 28 to 31.

Strasbourg Cathedral.

Nᵒˢ 33 to 35.

Chartres Cathedral.

Nᵒˢ 36 to 39.

Bourges Cathedral.

Nᵒˢ 32, 40, 41, 42.

Tournai Cathedral.

Painting on glass attained its highest excellence in the thirteenth century. The original simplicity and elevation of style was maintained during the fourteenth century, but in the fifteenth century its special characteristics were lost through excess of ornamentation. This may be noticed in the fragments selected from the cathedral of Tournai, the glass of which dates from 1475 to 1500.

MOYEN ÂGE

MIDDLE AGES.

XIII AND XIV CENTURIES.

TILES AND GLAZED FACINGS.

Until the twelfth century rich pavings and the facings of walls were made of mosaic work, or in compartments of coloured stones — such as jasper, porphyry, marble, etc., or of painted and enamelled stones.   In the thirteenth century glazed tiles were first used for this purpose.

The following is a plan of the numbers for which there is not space on the plate itself.

XIIIth CENTURY.

Nᵒˢ 1, 16, 17, 21, 25.

Cathedral of Laon.

Nᵒˢ 2, 3, 6, 7, 9, 10, 12, 13, 14, 15, 24, 31, 32, 33.

Museum of Rouen.

Nᵒ 4.

Abbey of Saint-Loup.

Nᵒˢ 5, 22, 27.

Cathedral of Saint-Omer.

Nᵒˢ 8, 19, 29.

Fontenay (Côte-d'Or).

Nᵒ 11.

Cluny Museum; Paris.

13	34	15	35	11	
16	17	36	13	37	19	20
33	21				7	6
22		38	30	41	23	
		39		42		
2	24	40	29	43	3	8
25	1				4	26
10		27		5	9	
32		12		31	
		11	28		

Nᵒ 18.

Reims; Hôtel de ville.

Nᵒˢ 20, 26.

Troyes.

Nᵒ 23.

Paris, Museum of the Louvre.

Nᵒ 28.

Troyes, Archives de l'Aube.

Nᵒ 30.

Rouen, Palais de Justice.

XIIIth AND XIVth CENTURIES.

Nᵒˢ 34 to 43.

Taken from various manuscripts in the Bibl. Nat.

N. B. The mean reduction is to the scale of one fourth.

The combinations adopted to secure economy in the manufacture of these tiles are extremely interesting to any one engaged in decoration. Our plate presents the varieties most in use.

Nᵒˢ 1 to 8.

1 Separate tile; complete design.

Nᵒˢ 9 to 12.

2 Tiles placed together horizontally, forming a border.

Nᵒˢ 13 to 29.

3 Tile varied in position four times four tiles together forming the whole pattern.

Nᵒ 30.

4 Hexagonal pavement, four pieces placed around a square, a new pattern.

Nᵒ 31.

5 Section of large pattern, consisting of nine tiles, and formed of three varieties.

Nᵒ 32.

6 Section of still larger pattern, consisting of sixteen tiles, and formed of four varieties.

Nᵒˢ 33 to 43.

7 Various single tiles.

Lith. par Wolfart.

Imp. Firmin-Didot fr. Fils & Cie Paris

MIDDLE AGES.

XV CENTURY.

EMBROIDERY AND DESIGNS FOR INLAYING.
FROM PAINTINGS.

This plate contains twenty-two examples of the decoration of hangings and stuffs, remarkable from their simplicity of design, which does not, however, exclude a striking effect. The designs consist of the union of gold with a single colour, either by placing the gold on a coloured ground, or, on the contrary, by stamping the pattern on a gold ground.

These twenty-two subjects are, for the most part, borrowed from different manuscripts in the *Bibliothèque nationale* at Paris. The following is a list of them with the numbers given in the plate.

Nos 1, 2, 3, 4, 5, 6.

Manuscript, B. N. French supplements. (No 542).

No 7.

Sainte-Chapelle de Bourbon-l'Archambault.

Nos 8, 9.

Window-glass from Moulins.

No 10.

Manuscript, B. N. (No 6,789).

No 11.

Manuscript of Monstrelet, B. N. (No 8,299.)

No 13.

Hours of Anne of Brittany (Louvre).

No 14.

Manuscript, B. N. (Colbert Collection, No 1174.)

No 15.

Manuscript, B. N. (No 540.)

Nos 16, 17.

Manuscript, B. N. (No 6,788.)

Nos 18, 19.

The Golden Legend, B. N. (No 6,888.)

Nos 20, 21.

Manuscript, B. N. (No 9,387. A. F.)

No 22.

Book of Hours of the Schœnborn Family, Manuscript belonging to M. de Rothschild.

Lithographié par Painlevé

Imp Firmin-Didot, fr Fils & C.ᵉ Paris

MIDDLE AGES.

XV CENTURY.

CONVENTIONAL FLORA AND FLOWER-WORK.

The details that fill the accompanying plate — too numerous for us to indicate the sources from which each is derived — have all been taken from manuscripts of the fifteenth century.

The subjects are, in general, taken from the European flora, sometimes in the simplest form, sometimes in arbitrary combinations of different plants with each other, or with figures of animals, and even with the human face.

The Middle Ages excelled in this sort of fantastic caprice, which may be varied to any amount by that freedom of imagination which characterises the style, but in which the principle of certain general forms stands out clearly. An example of this may be seen in the holly leaf — of such frequent use in manuscripts — and here presented under so many different aspects, and capable, even apart from illumination, of several applications. Amongst others we might suggest ornaments in iron-work.

MOYEN ÂGE

Lith. par Durin.

Imp. Firmin-Didot fr. Fils & Cie Paris

MIDDLE AGES.

XV CENTURY.

ILLUMINATIONS OF MANUSCRIPTS.

FLOWERS AND JEWELS.

The twenty-five subjects here represented are taken from various manuscripts, obtained from the following sources.

Nᵒˢ 1 and 2.

ILLUMINATED BOOK OF HOURS. (Bibl. Nat. MS. Nᵒ 1173; Colbert Coll. Nᵒ 4821.)

« The Latin text is dated 1398; the illuminations belong to a later time and may be attributed to Israel van Meckenen. »

Nᵒˢ 3 and 4.

LA LÉGENDE DORÉE (Bibl. Nat. MS. Nᵒ 6889), manuscript attributed to Jean Foucquet.

Nᵒˢ 5 and 6.

VARIOUS MANUSCRIPTS. (Library of the Arsenal.)

Nᵒ 7.

Book of Hours of the Shœnborn Family, belonging to M. de Rothschild.

Nᵒˢ 8 to 25.

Examples of jewellery, taken from the margin of a Seneca (Bibl. Nat. MS. Nᵒ 8551).

Although some details of the subjects given here are affected by the capricious and chimerical treatment so common in the middle ages, they have as a whole, a graceful and serious style, which allows of their being successfully imitated in modern times. From this point of view, we may especially notice the practical interest offered by the jewellery, Nᵒˢ 8 to 25.

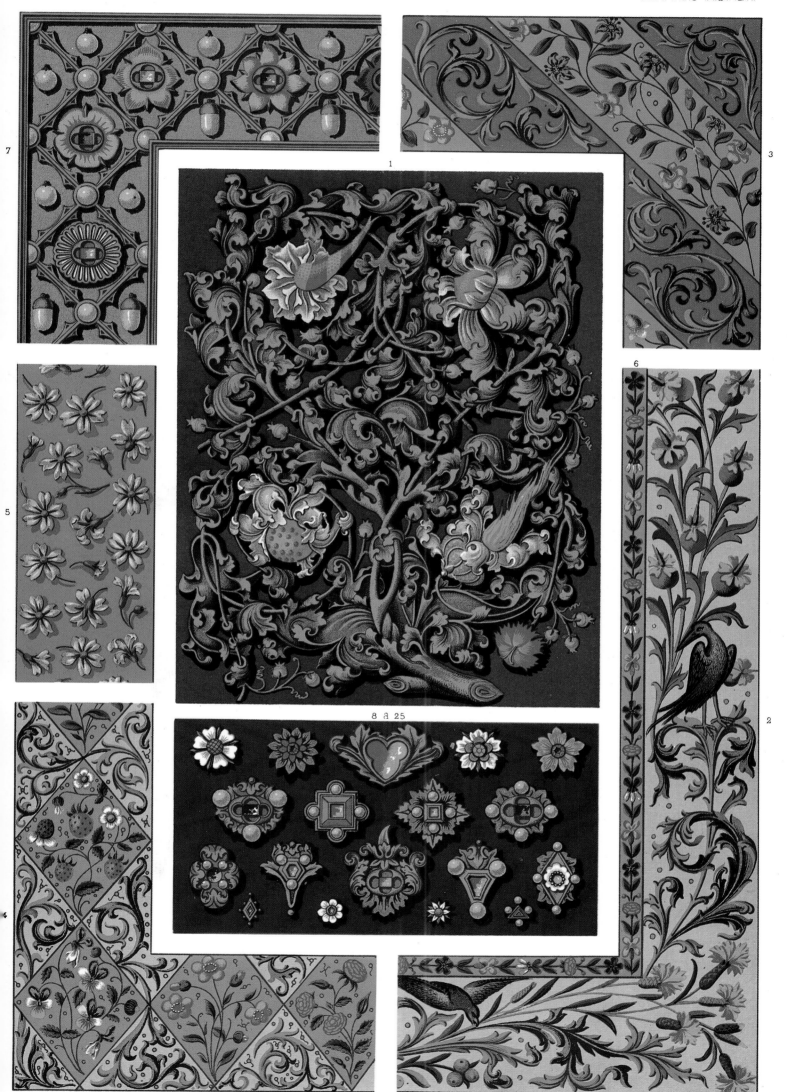

Lithographie par F. Durin.

Imp. Firmin-Didot fr. Fils & C.ᵉ Paris.

MIDDLE AGES.

XV CENTURY (SECOND PERIOD).

ILLUMINATIONS OF MANUSCRIPTS.

The illustrations contained in this plate may be taken as eminently original productions of the French and Flemish schools before the invasion of Italian art which characterized the time of the Renaissance properly so called. Natural objects such as branches, foliage, and flowers, are rendered in a decorative manner and with gracefulness, knowledge, and elegant variety.

Nᵒˢ 1 to 10.

BOOK OF HOURS of the *Marquis de Paulmy*.

Library of the Arsenal.

Nᵒˢ 11 and 12.

Manuscript belonging to the Comte de Bastard.

Nᵒˢ 13, 14.

ILLUMINATED HOURS attributed to Israel van Meckenen, Bibl. Nat. M. Sorb. 1173 ; Colbert collection, 4821.

Nᵒˢ 15 to 18.

VARIOUS MANUSCRIPTS.

Library of the Arsenal.

Lith. par F. Durin.

Imp. Firmin-Didot fr. Fils & Cie. Paris.

RENAISSANCE.

PANELS, FRIEZES, AND BORDERS.

All the specimens of which this plate is composed are taken from the famous book « *Heures à l'usage de Rouen, imprimées pour Symon Vostre, libraire demeurant à Paris,* » the first edition of which bears the date 1508.

The early monuments of the French Renaissance generally exhibit traces of their double origin. On one side they bear the impress of the essentially northern art which prevailed in France in the middle ages, and on the other they show the influence of the Italian style which was soon to carry all before it; here, however, the French style preponderates, and the Italian influence can only be noticed in a few of the subjects, especially those in the lower part of the plate.

Many of these simple subjects remind us of the charming ornamentation on beams still so frequently to be seen in old buildings in Normandy, Picardy, and Champagne.

Our ability to give our readers a representation in colour of this typographical work is only due to a trick which was frequently practised in the earlier times of printing, before the invention had been generally made known. The books of Symon Vostre, Vérard, and others, were frequently printed on vellum, and then painted like manuscripts, so as to conceal their true origin, and make the purchaser believe that he was acquiring an original manuscript. The copy, thus metamorphosed, of which we have made use, and the printing of which is entirely covered by colouring, as represented in the plate, has on it the arms of Jehan de Clisson, and forms part of the library of M. Ambroise Firmin Didot.

Lith. par Durin.

Imp. Firmin-Didot fr. fils & Cie. Paris

RENAISSANCE.

PAINTINGS ON MANUSCRIPTS.

All the specimens of which this plate is composed are taken from the Gradual of the Cathedral of Sienna, the ornamentation of which is by Girolamo da Cremona, one of the most fruitful artists of the close of the fifteenth century. Vasari speaks of him in the following terms, at the end of his life of Boccacino : « In his time there livedt at Milan a miniature painter named Girolamo, who produced works which are to be met with at Milan and throughout Lombardy ».

Girolamo da Cremona ranks among the best of miniature painters. His ornamentation is of a broad and powerful character, quite distinct from that of his contemporaries; it is a decided return towards the antique, but without detracting from the artist's originality. The ornamented ox's scull is interesting, and the monster with single head and double body is of the highest Grecian antiquity; indeed the architect Paccard has made use of this type in his restoration of the Parthenon.

RENAISSANCE

Bauer lith.

Imp. Firmin-Didot fr Fils & Cie, Paris.

RENAISSANCE.

XVI CENTURY.

FRESCOES AND ARABESQUES OF RAPHAEL.

LOGGIE OF THE VATICAN.

Everything that it is possible to say has already been said of these marvels of decoration, which are at the same time marvels of ideal art.   In giving a place in our collection to a few of these beautiful frescoes, executed, as is well known, under the direction of Raphael, by his principal pupils, we do not exceed the limits of our subject, but merely extend those limits by giving an example of the highest expression of which it is capable. These great works are more than mere decorations, but yet they *are* decorations, sometimes connected by unity of subject, sometimes abandoned, apparently, to the caprices of a charming fancy, but always subordinated to the general effect, and meeting in every respect the requirements of decorative art.

In the plate two large subjects occupy the right and left.   The former represents the Four Seasons, with their attributes expressed as clearly as poetically.   The latter shows the Three Fates, grand figures spinning between them the thread of human life.

The centre of the plate is filled with various examples from the same sources.

Lithog. par Painlevé.

Imp. Firmin-Didot fr Fils & Cie Paris.

PL. LIII.

XVI CENTURY.

DECORATIVE PAINTINGS IN THE VATICAN.

GROTESQUES.

« It is thought, » says M. Daussy, « that this expression was first applied to the imitations that were made of the figures of imaginary animals found in the fifteenth century in the subterraneous constructions, which the Italians term *grotte*. Grotesques result from the love of the marvellous, that imperious need of our nature to leave at times the human sphere and to soar away into the fairy land of imagination; this need is universal, it is born with man as much as poetry or thought, but it is developed most strongly in those nations in which the elements of civilisation are heterogeneous and produced by different causes.

« Rome naturally adopted the style which Raphael allegorized. »

(Histoire des Beaux-Arts, by Jacques Mérault-Daussy, 1849.)

All the fragments in the accompanying plate are from paintings by Raphael, except the trophy in the centre, which is by the hand of Giulio Clovio, and is taken from a manuscript in the Library of the Arsenal (H. F. N° 71, Réserve), and the two cameos in gold on a blue ground to the right and left of the example on a black ground in the lower part of the plate, which are from the *Casa Taverna* at Milan.

Lith par Durin

Imp. Firmin-Didot fr. Fils & Cⁱᵉ, Paris.

RENAISSANCE.

XVI CENTURY (FIRST PERIOD).

MINIATURES TAKEN FROM MANUSCRIPTS.

Of the five fragments contained in this plate the two first (N°s 1 and 2) decorate the frontispiece of a manuscript belonging to the Library of the Arsenal, Paris, entitled : *Historia romana excerpta ex libris historicis Pauli Orosii* (H. F. N° 71, Reserve).

These wonderful miniatures are by the Italian Giulio Clovio, a pupil of Raphael, whose great success is related by Vasari.

The characteristics of the Italian style, and especially of the school of Fontainebleau, may be seen in the other three fragments (N°s 3, 4 and 5), which are taken from a manuscript of Flavius Josephus in the Mazarin Library (Manuscripts, N° 518, H.).

5

1

2

4

Lithographié par Pralon.   Imp. Firmin Didot fr Fils & Cie Paris

RENAISSANCE

ENGRAVED IVORIES.

These engraved ivories come within the subject of polychromatic ornamentation by their combination of white and black.

Sometimes the black forms the background of the general design at other times it is used a as means of relieving and displaying the design.

In other specimens the pattern is drawn in black on the surface of the ivory by means of thin lines which are well relieved against the white background.

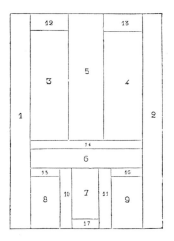

Nᵒˢ 1 to 4.

DETAILS of an ebony cabinet belonging to the Comte d'Yvon.

The panels and mounting of this magnificent cabinet were executed after the paintings of Raphael in the Vatican.

Nᵒ 5.

DETAILS of a chair belonging to M. Boulay de la Meurthe, also decorated after works in the Vatican engraved in outline.

Nᵒ 6.

EXAMPLES after Agostino of Venice.

Nᵒˢ 7 to 11.

EXAMPLES taken from the *Calcographie* of Comte Léopold Cicognara.

Nᵒˢ 12, 13.

Box belonging to M. Evans, dealer in curiosities.

Nᵒˢ 14 to 17.

SCROLL PATTERNS.

Lith. par Pralon.

FIRMIN DIDOT FRERES, FILS & C¹ᵉ EDITEURS

Imp. Lemercier & C¹ᵉ Paris

RENAISSANCE.

PAINTINGS ON MANUSCRIPTS,

AND FRESCOES.

The subjects represented in this plate belong to the Renaissance, the finest period of the art of the Italian minia-ture-painters. Vasari speaks with high praise of the three Florentine ornamentalists, Stefano, Gherardo, and Atta-vante or Vante, who specially distinguished themselves.

N° 1.

Missal for the dead, painted for Pope Paul II about 1450. (Chigi Library, at Rome.)

N° 2.

Manuscript from the library of Mathias Corvinus, painted by Attavante or Gherardo about 1492.

Nos 3, 4, 5, 6, 7.

Antiphonals from Florence, by Attavante; from 1526 to 1530.

Nos 8, 9.

Diurnal, large folio, signed Attavante di Gabriello.

Nos 10, 11.

Manuscript from the library of the Barberini Princes, at Rome, by Attavante.

Nos 12, 13.

Fragments of Raphael's decorative frescoes in the Vatican, probably painted by Giovanni da Udine, his pupil.

Nᵒˢ 14, 15.

Miniatures from the missal of Cardinal Cornari, attributed to Raphael.

Nᵒˢ 16, 17, 18, 19.

Lives of the Dukes of Urbino; (Vatican Library, at Rome.)

Nᵒˢ 20, 21, 22, 23, 24.

Horarum preces cum kalendario, Monasterii Terinent dated 1554, in the possession of M. Amb. Firmin Didot.

Imp Firmin-Didot.fr. Fils & C.ie, Paris

XIV CENTURY.

FIRST PERIOD.

CARTOUCHES.

The cartouche is especially an ornament of sculpture. The numerous modifications it has undergone should engage the attention of every artist. Adapting itself in its earlier stages to wood and leather work, cut and rolled in a thousand fashions, it afterwards appears in branches twisted like the letter S, and in the rock-work of the eighteenth century, resulting at last in the elegant forms of the Louis XVI period. The shield of the middle ages, surmounted by the helmet, with the scallop in various forms, was certainly the origin of it; but it was not until the fifteenth century that the Italians paid it the attention it deserved. This product of the architectural genius of European artists has nothing in common with the Oriental or Asiatic style; it settles the attention, and fixes interest by dividing it among the complicated patterns of which it is the principal motive, the other means of ornamentation being grouped around it in subordination.

Irrespective of numerous detached examples of cartouches, we give a sort of history of this style of composition in six plates which are placed in chronological order. We believe that this is now done for the first time.

N° 1.

XV CENTURY.

Example taken from a painting by Cima da Conegliano. (Louvre.)

N°s 2 to 5.

XVI CENTURY, 1st PERIOD.

Design by Antonio Razzi. (Louvre.)

N° 6.

Manuscript. (Library of the Arsenal, N° 328.)

N°s 7 to 11.

Enamelled terra-cotta in relief, Italian style. (Exterior decoration of the castle called the *Château de Madrid,* built by Francis I.)

N°s 12, 13, 14, 15, 18, 19, 20, 21.

Paintings of Primaticcio at Fontainebleau.

N°s 26, 27, 28.

Fragments of the ornamental borders of portraits, taken from a magnificent manuscript executed for Francis I, about 1530. (Bibl. Nat. French section, Réserve, N° 2848.)

N° 29.

Taken from a window in the ossuary of Saint-Étienne du Mont; French Renaissance, 1535.

This cartouche is one of the few relics of the Parisian Renaissance. It contained the arms of the donors of the windows, which were broken at the time of the Reformation; we have filled up the space they would have occupied by a contemporary arabesque.

N° 30.

Taken from a window with the arms of the corporation of goldsmiths of Rouen, dated 1543.

N°s 16, 17, 22, 23, 24, 25, 31 to 35.

Ornaments on manuscripts, from Geoffroy Tory, Cousin, etc.; time of Henry II.

RENAISSANCE.

ORNAMENTATION OF LIMOGES ENAMELS,

AND OF

ITALIAN EARTHENWARE.

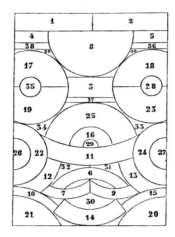

Painted enamel was brought into fashion by the old Limousin school about 1520, and attained its greatest perfection about 1540.   Il Rosso and Primaticcio painted cartoons for the Limousin enamellers, and thus assisted in the creation of this new species of jewellery.

Léonard, painter to Francis I, was the first superintendent of the Royal Manufactory of Enamel founded at Limoges by that King, and, on that account is frequently called Léonard Limousin. After him came Pierre Raymond, whose productions date from 1534 to 1578, the Pénicauds, Pierre and Jean Courteys, Martial Raymond, Mercier, and Jean Court, usually called *Vigier*.   (See M. Labarte, *Histoire des arts industriels,* and the annals of the studios given by M. Alfred Darcel in the *Notice des émaux et de l'orfévrerie, série D,* which is sold in the Louvre, Galerie d'Apollon.)

The fragments of ornamentation which we have collected are principally by Androuet du Cerceau, Jean Cousin, Pierre Woeiriot, and above all by Étienne de Laune, usually called *Stephanus,* who, as M. Paul Lacroix remarks (*Histoire de l'orfévrerie-joaillerie*), « had introduced, even in the greatest height of the Italian fever, a brilliant return to the schools of Jean Collaert of Antwerp, and of Théodore de Bry of Frankfort. »

This class of manufacture, the productions of which are now so costly, became very much depreciated towards the close of the sixteenth century, as we may see from l'*Art de terre* by Bernard Palissy. This eminent artist speaks of and deplores this decline of public taste; for, in his opinion, « no painting is so pleasing as these enamels well fused into the copper. » From this time forward enamellers began to make excessive use of spangles and gaudy colours, which were only employed in moderation by the founders of the school.

The specimens taken from the enamel manufactory at Limoges occupy Nᵒˢ 1 to 16 in our plate.

Nᵒˢ 1, 2, 3.
Enamels, by Martin Limousin.

Nᵒˢ 4, 5, 6.
From the studio of Léonard Limousin.

Nᵒ 7.
From the studio of Pierre Raymond.

Nᵒ 8.
Reverse of a tray, with the centre perforated, from the same.

Nᵒ 9.
Border from the same.

Nᵒˢ 10, 11, 12, 13.
Borders by Pierre Courteys.

Nᵒ 14.
Border and deepened edge attributed to Jean Courteys.

Nᵒ 15.
Border by Jehan Court, called *Vigier*.

Nᵒ 16.
By the same.

All these specimens are taken from the Louvre.

Nᵒˢ 17 to 40 represent fragments of Italian earthenware.

We cannot follow through all their varieties the productions of the manufactories at Pesaro, Gubbio, Urbino, Faenza, Rimini, Forli, Bologna, Ravenna, Ferrara, Cività-Castellana, Bassano, and Venice, by which the entire collection of Italian pottery was produced; the story of their competition with one another is extremely interesting. Although we give a few specimens of maiolica ware, we have not attempted the perfectly vain task of rendering exactly their beautiful metallic tints streaked with all the colours of the rainbow. We think, however, that it may be useful to represent some specimens of these decorations, the composition of which is frequently ingenious and always clear, whether they be derived from an oriental type or from Greek antiquity. Lanfranco, Giorgio Andreoli, Francesco, Xanto, Orazio Fontana, Guido Salvaggio, Flaminio Fontana, Battista Franco, and Raphael dal Colle are the principal authors of these works, although the first impulse was given to them by Luca della Robbia in the fifteenth century, and they were spread through Europe by the three brothers Giovanni, settled at Corfu, and by Guido of Savino, who took up his residence at Antwerp.

Some of these specimens are of such magnificence and beauty, that Christina of Sweden offered to exchange for them silver plate of the same size.

Nᵒˢ 17 to 23.
Dishes and borders of maiolica.

Nᵒˢ 24, 25.
Enamelled borders.

Nᵒˢ 26 to 29.
Camaieux.

Nᵒˢ 30 to 40.
Fragments in the grotesque style from the manufactories of Urbino.
Taken from the Museum of the Louvre and from private collections.

Jetot,lith.

Imp. Firmin-Didot fr. Fils & Cie Paris

PL. LIX.

RENAISSANCE.

ENAMELLED TILES.

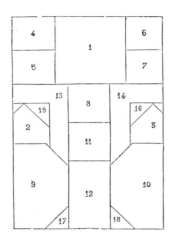

Nº 1.

Pentagonal tiles forming a pattern, from the collection of the Comte d'Yvon.

Nᵒˢ 2, 3.

Pentagonal tiles; the border, which is not given, is like that of Nº 1; from the same collection.

Nᵒˢ 4 to 8.

Tiles, the borders of all of which are the same as that of Nº 8; same collection.

Nᵒˢ 9 to 14.

Inlaid pavements, from the Château de Polisy (Aube).

Nᵒˢ 15 to 18.

Single tiles : from the same.

Lith. par Pralon
Imp.Firmin-Didot fr.Fils & Cⁱᵉ Paris.

RENAISSANCE.

PAINTING.

This painting on vellum, attributed to Giulio Clovio, was executed on the occasion of the elevation of Gregory XIII to the papal throne. It bears his name and arms, that is the arms of the Boncompagni family, and is dated 1573.

This fine decorative composition, which is a sort of compromise between the manuscript illuminations of the close of the fifteenth century, from which it borrows the use of natural figures of animals and flowers, and the more modern element of *cartouches* or scrolls, by the employment of these varied resources sustains the character for grandeur and harmony that characterized the school of Raphael to which the designer belonged.

The figures of the four Evangelists which occupy the centre of the composition, especially that of St John, are treated with a master's hand, and would be admired even without their admirable surroundings.

This painting belongs to M. Ambroise Firmin Didot.

GREGORIUS XIII
PONTIFEX OPTIMUS MAXIMUS
BONCOMPAGNUS BONONIENSIS
ELECTUS ANNO DOMINI M.D.LXXIII.

thogr. par Pralon   Imp. Firmin-Didot fr. Fils & Cie Paris

XVI AND XVII CENTURIES.

GOLD ENAMELLING AND JEWELLERY.

« Benvenuto Cellini, in his treatise on goldsmith's work, enters into minute technical and practical details on goldsmith's work in general, which he divides into eight distinct kinds : jewellery, niello, filigree work, chasing, intaglio, enamel, iron work, and the striking of medals and seals. In his opinion filigree, enamel, and iron work belong especially to the province of the French goldsmith. »

(*Histoire de l'orfévrerie-joaillerie*, by Paul Lacroix.)

The art of the goldsmith enameller is now lost; it began to decline from the time when Louis XIV had his plate melted down into coin in 1688; the use of porcelain and glass hastened its end. Henceforward it was only used for curiosities intended for presents, for which in 1698 the king still retained in the Louvre four goldsmiths : Mellin, Rotier, Delaunay, and Montarsy, and an enameller named Bain, « almost the only one in France at the present time, who has a thorough knowledge of transparent enamel, says Germain Brice in his *Description of Paris*.

Nos 1 and 2.
Chape of the scabbard of a sword, front and back.

No 3.
Ring of an oliphant, unfolded.

No 4.
Fragment from an agate vase.

Nos 5, 6, 7, 9, 12.
Fragments from a golden goblet.

Nos 8, 10, 14.
Setting of a clasp.

No 11.
Ring.

No 13.
End of a sword-hilt, from the treasury of the House of Austria.

No 15.
Mounting of a cameo on an ebony box.

Nos 16, 17.
Fragments of the same box from the ancient treasury of the kings of Poland, belonging to the Czartoryski family.

MUSEUM OF THE LOUVRE.

No 18.
Base of a vase mounted on a tripod.

Nos 19 to 26.
Handles of vases and goblets.

Nos 27 and 28.
Stands for goblets.

Nos 29 to 31.
Various fragments.

Lith par F. Durin.

Imp. Firmin-Didot fr. Fils & Cⁱᵉ Paris.

RENAISSANCE.

PAINTINGS ON MANUSCRIPTS.

The specimens contained in the accompanying plate are derived from two remarkable manuscripts, written in Spanish, forming part of the library of M. Ambroise Firmin Didot. The one comprises the grant of a patent of nobility to Juan Cataño in 1588, the other a similar grant to Augustin de Yturbe in 1593.

They give some idea of the effect produced in Spain by the Renaissance, to which period they must be referred.

The cartouche plays an important part in them, and usually serves as a frame surrounding human figures treated in a grotesque manner.

The broad and elegant style of the large initials, occuping the lower part of the plate, is especially worthy of notice.

Lith. par Bauër.   Imp. Firmin-Didot fr. fils & Cie, Paris

RENAISSANCE.

PAINTINGS ON MANUSCRIPTS.

The two superimposed subjects occupying the centre of the plate are of Italian origin and taken from the famous *Gradual of Sienna*.

All the others belong to the French Renaissance (School of Tours); they are of importance from their own merits as well as from the name of their author, François Colomb.

Michel Colomb or Columb, who built the sumptuous tomb, consecrated by the filial piety of Anne of Brittany to the memory of Francis II, last Duke of Brittany, and his wife Marguerite de Foix, was one of the most fertile of French artists. He died at the commencement of the sixteenth century.

We find in the old archives of Flanders, that Colomb was assisted by three nephews, « all perfect workmen, one in the carving of images, another in masonry, and the third in the art of illumination. The image carver was named Guillaume Regnault; the architect, Bastyen François; the illuminator, François Colomb. Colomb himself prepared the models in terra cotta »; Bastyen François was entrusted with the architectural part of the monument; and afterwards François Colomb decorated the models with painting according as the colour of the material required, « flesh-tints for face and hands, inscriptions, and every thing else belonging thereto. » (See *Nantes*, by the Baron de Guillermy; Annales archéologiques de Didron, 1845.)

This account gives great interest to the adjoined specimens, which are taken from a manuscript in the *Bibliothèque Nationale*, Latin Section N° 886; in them may be recognized all the features noticed in the above description, and the peculiar taste and style of the Colombs.

RENAISSANCE.

CEILING WITH GILDED COMPARTMENTS.

The oak ceiling with carved and gilded compartments represented in the plate, is that of the large hall of the Parliament of Normandy (now the Court of Assizes), which is to be seen in the *Palais de Justice* at Rouen.

The special books written on this building tell us neither the designer of this beautiful ceiling, nor the precise date that may be assigned to it. We may however consider it as contemporaneous with the rest of the palace, since this building, commenced by Louis XII and the Cardinal d'Amboise about 1499, — the time at which the Norman Court of Exchequer was rendered permanent, — was considered almost complete in 1514. The general style of the decoration, also, would seem to belong to the same period, i. e. the beginning of the sixteenth century or the commencement of the Renaissance.

We do not think that this work of art, so well known and so generally admired, has ever before been reproduced in a complete manner, and especially with colouring; we are therefore happy to be able to present it to our readers.

In the present state of the original, the oak wood which forms the ground, has become almost black; it was thought best to give it as far as possible its original colour.

BIBLIOGRAPHY OF THE SUBJECT.

ACH. DEVILLE. *Précis analytique des travaux de l'Académie de Rouen*; 1840.

FLOQUET. *Histoire du Parlement*; Frère, 1840.

JOLIMONT; *Les principaux édifices de la ville de Rouen en 1525*; Rouen, 1845.

DE STABENRATH. *Notice sur le Palais de Justice de Rouen.* Edet, 1843.

Lith par Dufour et Laval

Imp Firmin-Didot fr. Fils & Cⁱᵉ Paris.

RENAISSANCE.

XVI CENTURY.

DECORATIVE PAINTING AND SCULPTURE.
FROM FRENCH MONUMENTS.

If there is one period more interesting than another in the history of French national art, it is certainly that, in which French artists, under the foreign influence which was beginning to predominate, added the spirit of Italian art to their own natural taste.

In the present day justice is rendered to this national school, which had been wonderfully prepared by its solid studies and strong originality for the lessons of ancient art at that time so enthusiastically received.

« From 1460, » says Jeanron (*Recherches sur l'origine et les progrès de l'art*), « our artists began to show at once an original style, peculiar taste, and « deep appreciation of the models of antiquity.   Their personal inspiration and free interpretation assigned them a high rank in the movement « called the Renaissance.... We will not allow it to be said, on the faith of literary exaggerations, that the Italian artists summoned to the court of « Francis I, taught their art to low and ignorant French artists. The rapid way, in which our national school appropriated the Italian manne « proves, on the contrary, its advancement and strength. »

The examples in our plate are derived from the following sources :

N°s 1, 2, 3.
Stone sculptures; château de Blois, 1530.

N°s 4 to 7.
Stone sculptures; château de Châteaudun, 1530.

N°s 8 to 15.
Wood carving; château de Blois, 1530.

N°s 16 to 19.
Wood carving; château de Blois (oratory of Catherine de Médicis), 1560.

N°s 20 to 24.
Painting on manuscripts derived from :
1° The Bible of the Arsenal;
2° Book of Hours of the Schoenborn family. M. de Rothschild.

Lith. par G. Sanier

Imp. Firmn-Didot fr. Fils & C?, Paris.

RENAISSANCE.

ENAMELLED EARTHENWARE.

The dishes and borders contained in this plate are specimens of the workmanship of Bernard Palissy.

This active and industrious experimentalist spent many years in arduous toil, before he succeeded in discovering the secret of the Oriental and Italian productions, which he wished to imitate. We are unable to devote any space to the representation of those minute figures of natural objects for which he was so celebrated. These constitute a separate syle which, notwithstanding its success, exercised no decisive influence over the general taste of the period. His other works, inspired by the productions of Prieur, Germain Pilon and Jean Goujon, are in the same style as those of his contemporaries, and it is to this phase of his talent that the subjects represented in our plate belong.

The ornamental dish, occupying the upper part of the plate, was mounted on tin, in the manner then recently brought into fashion by the goldsmiths of the period. It was designed by François Briot, from whom Palissy frequently borrowed subjects. All these examples are taken from the Museums of the Louvre and of Cluny.

Lith par Durin.

FIRMIN-DIDOT-FRÈRES FILS & Cⁱᵉ ÉDITEURS

Imp.Testu & Massin,Paris.

RENAISSANCE.

BINDINGS, AND VENETIAN MARQUETRY.

Nº 1.

Specimen of binding, the centre of which is occupied by an oil painting, here merely sketched in outline.

Nº 2.

Specimen of binding, with the inside border.

These two fine specimens are from the library of M. Ambroise Firmin Didot.

Nº 3.

Three specimens of marquetry from a harpsichord of the sixteenth century (Cluny Museum).

In all these specimens the designs are essentially Persian, and they form a fitting sequel to our examples of Oriental ornamentation. Our object in placing them under the title *Renaissance* has been to show the part that Venice, through its constant relations with the Levant, took in the introduction of the arabesque, which ornament, since the sixteenth century, has been so happily blended with the Greco-Roman tradition.

Lith par Lemoine   Imp. Firmin-Didot fr. Fils & Cᵉ Paris

Pl. LXVIII.

XVI AND XVII CENTURIES.

SPECIMENS OF INLAID BINDINGS.

One of the most interesting branches of ornamental art is undoubtedly that of the binder. The taste for handsome bindings, a natural accompaniment to the passion for fine books and rare editions, has from the earliest time caused the production of masterpieces, which we think it well to bring before the notice of our readers.

For this plate we have chosen models which, by the combined use of colours and gold, come especially within the limits of our subject. The following are the sources from which they have been obtained :

Nº 1.

A copy of Procopius, *De Bello Persico*, 4ᵗᵒ, 1509.
This handsome Italian binding was made for Maioli the celebrated collector of books, and bears this inscription : *Th. Maioli et amicorum.*
Library of M. Ambroise Firmin Didot.

Nº 2.

A copy of the edition of Paul Jovius, folio, Florence, 1549.
This copy comes from the well-known library of Grolier and bears the inscription : *Grollerii et amicorum.*
Library of M. Ambroise Firmin Didot.

Nº 3.

A copy of the Bible of R. Stephanus, folio, Paris, 1540.
« The binding was executed for the President de Thou and appears to have formed a part of his library. »
Library of M. Ambroise Firmin Didot.

Nº 4.

Commentary on the Pentateuch, 4ᵗᵒ.
Bibliothèque Nationale (Saint-Germain français, 4).

Nº 5.

Corner of the cover of a book with the arms of Henry II and the initials of Diana of Poitiers.
Mazarin Library.

Nº 6.

Another specimen with the arms of Henry II and the initials of Diana of Poitiers.
This work bears as its title : *Fl. Vegetii, Renati viri, et.....*
Mazarin Library.

Nº 7.

Biblia *ex duplici versione altera Vulgata, altera Tigurina Leonis de Juda, cum annotationibus Fr. Vatabli. Lutetiæ, ex officina Rob. Stephani,* 1545, 2 vols. 8ᵛᵒ, red morocco, inlaid, gilt edges.

This binding is thus described in the catalogue of the sale of M. Brunet's books, under number 2 :

« A rich and elegant binding of the sixteenth century with inlaid compartments, as remarkable fro its good preservation as for its beauty.

« This copy is the one offered by Jean Grolier to the president Christophe de Thou, and at his death it passed to his son Jacques-Auguste de Thou, the well known historian. In 1789, it formed part of the collection of the Prince de Soubise, to which, as is well known, that of J. A. de Thou had been united. Le Roux de Lincy alludes to it in p. 93 of his work on Grolier, but he did not know what had become of the book; I obtained it at the sale that took place after the death of Renouard but without knowing its history, which the work of M. de Lincy has recently revealed to me. This magnificent binding is still in the most perfect preservation, and very different in that respect from the Hippocrates of the Motteley collection, of which the back was restored in the eighteenth century and the sides only imperfectly repaired. »
(Note of M. Brunet.)

Nº 8.

Heures de la Vierge, 8ᵛᵒ. Paris, Guillaume Merlin, 1555.
Library of M. Ambroise Firmin Didot.

Nº 9.

Back of a volume with the arms of Henry II.
Mazarin Library.

Nº 10.

Roman Missal, folio, Venetiis, Ant. de Zanchis, 1506.
The binding is Italian and of a later period, having been executed at the beginning of the seventeenth century.
Collection of M. Bachelin-Deflorenne.

Nº 11.

Grandes Annales et Chroniques d'Angleterre, by Jean Besnard, formerly secretary of the queen of England (completed March 22ⁿᵈ 1567, and dedicated to the king of France, Charles IX, by the author).
It is the fore-edge of the volume that is given in our plate.
Bibl. Nat. (French manuscripts nº 5575.)

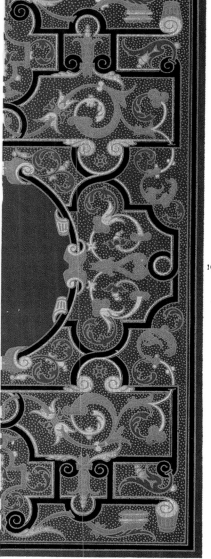

Lith par Pralon   Imp. Firmin-Didot fr. Fils & Cie Paris

XVI CENTURY.

PAINTINGS ON MANUSCRIPTS, AND DAMASKEENINGS.

The first seven numbers represent paintings from a manuscript executed for Henry II (*Confirmation des priviléges des notaires et secrétaires par Louis XI*). It is one of the finest specimens of the ornamentation of that period. The resemblance of these paintings to undoubted works of Jean Cousin leaves us scarcely any room for doubt in attributing them to that artist.

The volume forms part of the library of M. Ambroise Firmin Didot.

The specimens marked 8 and 9 are by Androuet du Cerceau and are of the same class as the old paintings at Fontainebleau.

N°s 10 to 15 represent designs of damaskeening taken from the masterpieces of the Lyons press. These also are in the library of M. Ambroise Firmin Didot.

Lith par Picard

Imp. Firmin-Didot fr. Fils & Cie. Paris.

XVI CENTURY.

CARTOUCHES ON FRIEZES, SCROLLS, AND ORNAMENTAL NAILS.

This plate contains forty-four examples. That with a green ground, on which the initials of Henry and Catherine are to be seen, is taken from the decoration of the beams in the oratory of Catherine de Medici in the Château de Chenonceaux.

The pendentive on a yellow ground, placed under the preceding subject at the lower part of the plate, is taken from a fresco painting in the Chapel of the same castle.

The forty two remaining subjects, which are likewise unnumbered, come from the historical gallery of Thevet, entitled : *Les Vrais portraits et vies des hommes illustres, grecs, latins et payens, recueillis de leurs portraits, livres, médalles, antiques et modernes,* Paris, 1584.

This valuable collection of full-length portraits, engraved on copper towards the close of the sixteenth century, is particularly rich in architectural decorations of a unique type, the details of which vary in every page. To accomplish this immense work it was necessary to use almost every suitable specimen in existence. Some idea of its extent may be formed from the rich collection contained in the accompanying plate, selected from a copy which was coloured at the time of its publication.

Lith. par Pralon   Imp. Firmin-Didot fr Fils &Cie Paris.

XVI AND XVII CENTURIES (FIRST PERIOD).

CARTOUCHES.

It is interesting to follow the development of the cartouche through the various phases of French national art. The examples given here belong to the second part of sixteenth century and to the first part of the following one.

Numbers 1 to 4 are taken from a manuscript in the Library of the Arsenal, attributed to Jean Cousin.

The rest are, for the most part, of Flemish origin and come from different sources. They are mostly ornaments of maps, but are capable of different applications, especially in the common use of wood and leather as materials for ornamentation.

Lith. par Krautz & Sauer   Imp. Firmin-Didot Fr. Fils & Cⁱᵉ Paris

XVI AND XVII CENTURIES.

EMBROIDERED HANGINGS.

The examples given in our plate have been obtained from two different sources.

Nᵒˢ 1 and 2.

Collection of M. Bouvier, painter.

In these two fragments, brought from Genoa, the embroidery is of cloth on a ground of the same material, and the borders alone are of silk.

Nᵒ 3.

Collection of M. Leclercq, dealer in curiosities, Paris.

In the third example, the ground is of silk figured with violet on violet (Lyons style) and the embroideries are in yellow satin. It is from Milan.

The designs, which are of great firmness, are remarkable for their powerful relief, which would almost render them fit subjects for ornamental sculpture. They are worthy of the best masters of the time.

Lith. par Dufour & F. Durin   Imp. Lemercier & Cⁱᵉ Paris

XVII CENTURY.

PAINTINGS, CARVINGS, AND OPEN WORK.

The various fragments collected in this plate all belong to the same period, and to the style usually called after Louis XIII, as is shown by the source from which N° 7 is drawn.

N° 1.

Fragment of wood inlaid with carved ivory and mother of pearl, the size of the original, belonging to the Comte d'Yvon, and dated 1598.

This carving, of which it is not easy to guess the use, is extremely delicate and intricate, and was probably executed to procure admission to a guild.

Nos 2, 3.

Silver frames, pierced and chased, of the size of the original, dating from the beginning of the century; communicated by M. Mayor.

N° 4.

A frieze from the pavilion of the two Queen-Mothers at Fontainebleau. Time of Louis XIII.

N° 5.

Cipher of Louis XIII and Anne of Austria. (From the same.)

N° 6.

Upper part of the left wing of the gilded door at Fontainebleau, before restoration.

N° 7.

Casket of Anne of Austria, in chased gold, on a velvet ground. (Louvre.)

Lith par G Sauier   FIRMIN-DIDOT FRERES, FILS & Cᵗᵉ EDITEURS.   Imp Lemercier & Cᵗᵉ Paris

XVII CENTURY.

FIRST PERIOD (STYLE LOUIS XIII).

PANEL OF GILT LEATHER WITH BORDER.

The accompanying plate represents one of the finest specimens of the manufacture of ornamental leather, (stamped with patterns in gold and silver,) which flourished in the sixteenth and seventeenth centuries. The name *Cordovan leather,* frequently given to these productions, would seem to indicate a Spanish origin, though it is far from being proved. It was from Venice, where the idea originated in the imitation of the rich brocades from the East, and also from England, Holland, and Flanders (particularly Malines) that these rich hangings were brought. Some manufactories of them also existed at Lyons.

These leathers, made from calf, goat or sheep skin, treated like ordinary sheep-skin after having been in the tan, and having drawings or paintings stamped upon them, were always silvered before gilding, which latter process was effected by a varnish imitating gold.

These hangings justly enjoyed great favour as they were very durable, being impervious to damp and other causes of decay, and the effort made by modern trade to bring them once more into fashion is worthy of encouragement.

The one represented in our plate is in the Cluny Museum (N° 1715 in the Catalogue).

Lithographié par Sanier.

Imp. Lemercier & Cie Paris

XVII CENTURY (FIRST PERIOD).

MURAL PAINTINGS, MINIATURES, ENAMELS, AND ENGRAVINGS IN NIELLO.

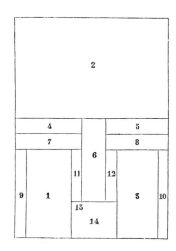

N° 1.

Panel from the pavilion of the Queen-Mothers at Fontainebleau.

N° 2.

Panel of the painted ceiling in the apartment of Anne of Austria in the Palace of the Louvre.

N° 3.

Panel copied from the Luxembourg Palace.

Nos 4, 5.

Miniatures taken from a manuscript executed for Anne of Austria. Mazarin Library.

Nos 6 to 12.

Decorative paintings of the architecture of Saint-Eustache, published by A. Lenoir. (*Statistique monumentale de Paris.*)

Nos 13, 14.

Fragments of gold enamel and of engravings in niello.

Lithographié par Launay.

Imp. Firmin-Didot fr. Fils Cie Paris.

XVII CENTURY (FIRST PART).

CARTOUCHES, CONFINED AND FREE.

N⁰ˢ 1, 2, 3, 4 come from the panels and roof of the Chapelle d'Hinisdal of the bare-footed Carmelites, after A. Lenoir (*Statistique monumentale de Paris*). These fragments belong to the first half of the century.

The separate cartouches are all taken from ornaments on maps, many of which date as far back as 1645. They were engraved in Flanders, and the colouring is merely tinsel.

N⁰ˢ 5 and 6 are taken from Bernardus Castellus.

The masks and intercalated branches are also of Flemish origin, belong to the same period, and are taken from Jean Christophe Feinlin.

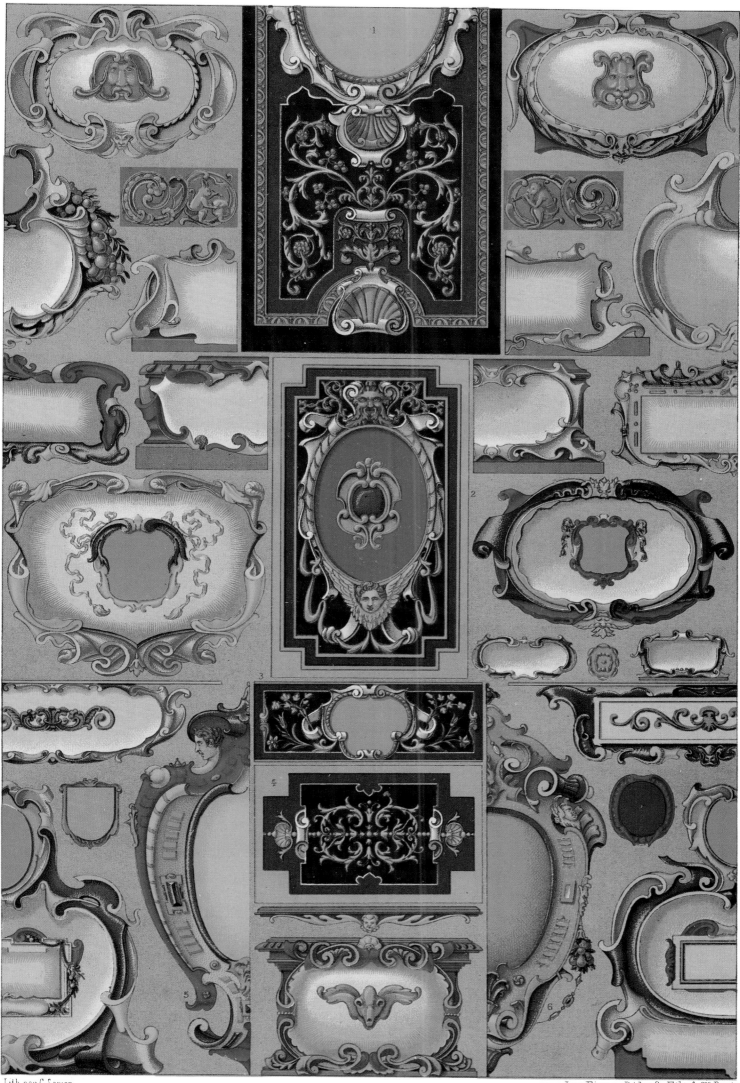

Lith par C. Sauer.   Imp. Firmin-Didot fr. Fils & Cⁱᵉ Paris.

PL. LXXVII.

XVII CENTURY.

FIRST PERIOD.

HANGINGS, EMBROIDERY, AND DAMASKEENING.

In this plate a certain number of subjects have been collected, derived from various sources and of different uses but to some extent similar in character. The examples have been obtained as follows.

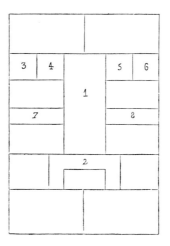

N° 1.

LEATHER HANGINGS, from the Château de Cheverny, near Blois (1635).

N° 2.

WOODEN FRAME, INLAID WITH METAL, from Touraine (same period).

N°ˢ 3 to 8.

DAMASKEENING OF THE FLEMISH STYLE, after Jean Christophe Feinlin.

All the other specimens are German embroideries, the designs on which have a sufficiently striking resemblance to those published by Hans Friedrich Raidel at Ulm (in 1613) to warrant us in attributing them to that artist.

The necessity of greatly reducing these interesting specimens has compelled us, in order to preserve their clearness, to change the deep grounds on which the embroidery was often laid for lighter ones. The high relief of these ornaments is shown to great advantage on white silk, and on red, crimson, or dark green velvet, as may be seen in the Cluny Museum. (*Salle des tentures et étoffes,* first case to the left on entering.)

Lith. par Dufour & Durin.

Imp. Firmin-Didot fr. Fils & Cⁱᵉ Paris

XVII CENTURY.

DECORATIVE PAINTINGS.

PANELS TAKEN FROM THE APOLLO GALLERY IN THE LOUVRE.

AFTER BÉRAIN.

The two principal subjects in this plate form part of the decoration of the window named after Charles IX.

« Bérain, » says Mariette, « cabinet-maker in ordinary to the king of France, was much employed in making designs for furniture, and ornaments to be executed in tapestry or painted on wainscotings and ceilings, of the kind called *grotesques*. — He selected from amongst the works that Raphael had so judiciously adapted from the antique those which appeared to him to produce the best effect. He reproduced them in a style suited to French taste and was so successful that even foreigners adopted his method of ornamentation. »

These compositions, much in vogue during the latter part of the seventeenth century, were at that time called *Bérinades*.

(See Destailleur, *Notice sur quelques artistes français*.)

Dufour et Picart lith.

FIRMIN-DIDOT FRÈRES FILS & Cie ÉDITEURS.

Imp. Lemercier & Cie Paris.

XVII CENTURY.

SECOND PERIOD.

ARCHED CEILING.

This plate represents a reduction of a gilded ceiling in the ancient Hôtel de Mailly, situated in Paris, at the corner of the Quai Voltaire and Rue de Beaune (see *Plan de Turgot,* and *Nouvelle description de Paris* by Germain Brice, 1725, p. 145), and recently occupied by the Cercle Agricole.

Adorned in the rich and elegant taste which prevailed at the close of the seventeenth century, this remarkable work is worthy of the best masters of that period, Bérain or Daniel Marot, and may justly be ascribed to the latter, or to his school. In the engraved works of Marot (*Nouveau livre de peintures de salles et d'escaliers,* 1712, p. 36), there is another ceiling, the striking similarity of which would support this conjecture.

Lithographié par Pralon

Imp. Firmin-Didot fr. Fils & Cie Paris.

XVII CENTURY.

MOSAIC, AND PAINTINGS.

Nº 1.

Fragment of a ceiling at Versailles painted by Mignard; now destroyed.

Nº 2.

Fragment of grand staircase at Versailles, by Lebrun; destroyed.

Nº 3.

Fragment of grand gallery at Versailles, by Lebrun.

Nº 4.

Design for the top of a table in marble mosaic, attributed to Robert de Cotte (Bibl. Nat., *Cabinet des Estampes*).

The four painted borders are from a house in the Rue de Beaune, and from the drawing-room, the ceiling of which is represented in plate ; the decorations may be attributed to Daniel Marot.

Lith par Durin   Imp. Firmin-Didot fr. Fils Cⁱᵉ Paris

PL. LXXXI.

XVII AND XVIII CENTURIES.

EARTHENWARE.

FRENCH MANUFACTURE.

The accompanying plate contains a certain number of specimens of French earthenware. They may be thus classed :

It was only about the middle of the sevententh century that the first manufactories of earthenware were established at Rouen, under the protection of Colbert. His patronage procured for them the privilege of working for the king, rom the designs of the best artists of the period. Those of our readers who are curious to learn the history and vicissitudes of this remarkable art may consult with profit the interesting monograph entitled, *Histoire de la Faïence de Rouen,* a posthumous work of M. André Pottier, keeper of the Public Library and Keramic Museum at Rouen, published under the care of the Abbé Collas, and of Messrs Gustave Gouellain and Raymond Bordeaux, *First part, Rouen,* 1869.

The specimens that we have chosen, as belonging to the best periods of the manufacture, are nearly all to be ound in the Cluny Museum.

Lith. par Dufour & Jeanningros   Imp. Firmin-Didot fr. Fils & Cie Paris

XVII CENTURY.

TAPESTRIES AND BORDERS.

The principal subject in the accompanying plate, with its border (N°s 1 and 2), is taken from a most beautifully designed piece of tapestry in the Château de Grignan.

Numbers 3 and 4 belong, to judge from the style and costumes, to a period nearer to the eighteenth century. The one which contains the two shepherdesses, designed after the fashion then prevalent, belongs to a series representing the twelve months of the year, in which it takes the place of June, characterised by the sheep-shearing and the sign of Cancer, the small size of which in the original does not allow of its being represented in the reduced proportions of our plate.

Between these last fragments and the tapestry of the Château de Grignan a difference of execution exists which is worthy of being noted. In the latter the colouring is flat; in the others the outline of the ornament is determine- by lighter tints on a dark background, and by darker ones on a light ground; the latter system being most fred quently adopted in the designs for prints and chintzes.

XVII AND XVIII CENTURIES.

INLAID WORK — BOULLE.

The *genre Boulle*, one of those manufactures which have conferred the greatest honour on France, has now regained the favour it enjoyed at the close of the seventeenth and commencement of the eighteenth centuries.

André Charles Boulle (born in 1642, died aged 90 in 1732) applied to cabinet-work all the faculties of a true artist. Appointed first cabinet-maker to the king by a patent which gave him the triple title of architect, sculptor, and engraver; he was lodged in the Louvre, and made one of the richest collections then known, of drawings, engravings, and works of art, a part of which was unhappily destroyed by fire, and the rest sold at the instance of creditors. The possession of such valuable materials explains, in part, the perfection of the original works which came from the master's hand. Boulle founded a school and gave his name to the *genre*, which was afterwards continued by Caffieri and Crescent, and is still successfully imitated.

This kind of art, which is not merely distinguished by the beauty and richness of its designs, but also for the happy combination of woods of various colours or of different metals, belongs essentially to polychromatic decoration.

The specimens given in our plate come from four different sources.

Nᵒˢ 1 to 5.

UPRIGHT CLOCK, with copper ground and tortoise-shell ornaments.

In this piece the silvery effect shown the copper ground, as on in our plate, is obtained by means of a particular varnish, spread over the copper, which gives tints of silver and mother of pearl.

Mazarin Library.

Nᵒˢ 6 to 10.

CABINETS IN MARQUETRY, tortoise-shell ground with ornaments of engraved copper.

Mazarin Library.

Nᵒˢ 10 to 14.

GENERAL VIEW AND DETAILS OF A VERY FINE LOUIS XIV piece of furniture, of great size, in ebony with copper ornaments representing as the principal subject, « Hercules overthrowing the Hydra of Lerna ».

This piece of furniture forms a part of the collection of M. Mannheim, to whose kindness we are indebted for our illustration.

Nᵒˢ 15 to 17.

VARIOUS SPECIMENS OF ORNAMENTATION in marquetry.

XVII CENTURY.

SILK AND STAMPED DESIGNS.

These two productions, which as regards colour are so extremely simple, belong to the close of the seventeenth century.

The exquisite design of the specimen of silk, which occupies the upper part of the plate, is in the Franco-oriental style, which an already widely spread knowledge of Persian ornamentation had established in France. The arrangement of vertical bars, forming stripes in the material from top to bottom, is highly decorative. This beautiful design, formed merely by the judicious distribution of one colour, contrasts agreeably with the more pretentious decorations of the period.

The subject in the lower part of the plate is taken from a stamped book-cover, of which it forms the inside ornament, in the style already in use under Louis XIII. The arrangement of the ornamentation belongs to the school of the Bérains, Marots, etc. Branches in double lines, producing acanthus leaves, from which depend small clusters of grapes, compose all its elements.

Lith par Leveil   Imp.Firmin-Didot fr Fils & Cie, Paris.

XVII AND XVIII CENTURIES.

GILDED LEATHER AND BORDERS.

We have already given some explanation as to the origin and manufacture of these stamped leathers, with ornaments printed in gold and colours. (See pl. .)

Here the great variety of tints and the use of more delicate colours than those employed in the Louis XIII style characterise the more coquettish and mannered, but at the same time intelligent period of art with which the eighteenth century opened.

The beauty of the ornaments will astonish no one, if it be borne in mind that for this most costly luxury the designs were usually obtained from the best decorative artists of the time, such as Oppenord, and the Meissonniers.

Nᵒˢ 1 and 2.
Cluny Museum.

Nᵒˢ 3 to 7.
COLLECTION OF M. LECLERCQ, dealer in curiosities, Paris.

Nᵒ 8.

COLLECTION OF M. RÉCAPPÉ.

Lith par Dufour & F. Durin

Imp. Firmin-Didot Fr. Fils & Cie Paris

XVII CENTURY.

LOUIS XIV STYLE.

CARPETS.

The carpet-pattern represented in our plate forms part of the manuscript work of Robert de Cotte (Bibl. Nat., *Cabinet des Estampes*, N° 9).

Robert de Cotte (1657-1735), brother-in-law and pupil of Mansart, enjoyed a high reputation as an architect during the reign of Louis XIV. The completion of the Chapel at Versailles, the Ionic colonnade at Trianon, the fountain in the square of the Palais-Royal (destroyed in 1848), the gallery of the Hôtel de la Vrillière (now the Bank of France), and the plans for the Place Bellecour at Lyons, of the Abbey of Saint-Denis, and of the doorway of Saint-Roch at Paris, are among his principal works.

To show the value of his talent as a decorator, we cannot do better than quote what M. Destailleur says of him in his *Notices sur quelques artistes français* (Paris, 1863, Rapilly) :

« Robert de Cotte, brother-in-law of Mansart, and early associated in all the great works of the time, became his successor....

« No one was more capable than he of directing the movement which took place in the decorative arts immediately after the death of Louis XIV...

« In the decoration of the Hôtel de Toulouse (1713-1719) Robert de Cotte showed what could be made of the old and also of the new style destined to take the name of Louis XV....

« The ornamentation he employs, whilst preserving the grandeur of the Louis XIV style, is treated with a certain freedom in the details, which renders it quite captivating. »

XVIII CENTURY.

TAPESTRIES.

These six specimens of tapestry form a continuation to plate V and are selected from the work of Robert de Cotte (Bibl. Nat., *Cabinet des estampes*).

We have nothing in particular to notice concerning them, except that it seems to us that the four examples in the lower part of the plate cannot be attributed to the same hand as the other two, which are by the author of the magnificent tapestry represented in the plate we have just spoken of.

With this reservation, they may all be attributed to the same school, which is characterised by a degree of architectural arrangement and an imposing richness of ornamentation.

Lith par Bauer   Imp.Firmin-Didot fr. Fils & Cie Paris

XVII AND XVIII CENTURIES.

TAPESTRIES.

We do not hesitate to attribute these beautiful Gobelins tapestries — so eminently French in their style — to Gillot, the master of Watteau, who, as is well known, was frequently employed in works of this kind (1).

The subject in the centre (N° 5) is the back of an arm-chair, which appears to have formed a part of a set, the subjects for which were drawn from the Fables of La Fontaine. It represents the Oak and the Reed.

In the other fragments, we find intermixed with various symbols, treated in a masterly way, some half serious, half grotesque, yet striking figures, the strange type of which, in accordance with what was then the prevailing idea entertained respecting Barbarous and Asiatic nations, reminds one of the grand serio-comic ceremonies of the fêtes at Versailles or at Sceaux.

N°ˢ 1, 2, 3, are consecutive and together make a complete border.

The reader may remark as typical of this manufacture the enlargement and isolation of a lower border (N° 6) by the use of a raised foreground, representing in this instance foliage *en espalier,* and the same effect is obtained for the upper border (N° 4) by the assistance of ornaments hanging from it.

(1) These tapestries form a part of the collection of M. Leclercq, dealer in curiosities, Paris.

Lith·par C. Sauer.   Imp.Firmin-Didot fr. Fils & Cie Paris.

XVIII CENTURY.

DECORATIVE PAINTING.

The ceiling represented in this plate belongs to the earlier part of the eighteenth century.

It is painted in camaieu and decorates the bath-room of a house at Versailles, formerly the residence of the Princess de Conti, daughter of Louis XIV and Mad^{me} de Lavallière; it bears her initials.

We are indebted to M. Eudore Soulié, Keeper of the Museum of Versailles, for a knowledge of this charming work, belonging to an interesting period of French ornamentation, and painted in all its details by the hand of a master.

The house, of which this ceiling forms a part, is situated in the Avenue de Sceaux, and is now a private dwelling.

Lith. par Dufour et Pralon

FIRMIN-DIDOT FRÈRES FILS & Cie EDITEURS

Imp. J. Chéret, 18, r. Brunel, Paris.

XVIII CENTURY.

DECORATIVE PAINTING.

This plate is composed of fragments, the varied repetitions of which form nearly the entire decoration of a harpsichord manufactured in the first part of the eighteenth century.

This magnificent piece of furniture is in the Cluny Museum. The ornaments are painted on gilded wood; and the fantastic design, which characterises it, is in the favourite style of Gillot, and Watteau.

The two fragments in the upper part unite at the green upright, where one finishes and the other commences the bower forms the centre of the design, and the other groups are repeated on each side, variations of the figures and of the garlands of flowers completing the frieze.

The lower part of the plate represents the decoration of the front of the harpsichord.

XVIII CENTURY.

TAPESTRIES, BINDINGS, AND WOOD-WORK.

The two large specimens occupying the upper part of our plate are tapestries of Beauvais manufacture, from the collection of M. Léopold Double.

These borders, which are imitated from a copy of La Fontaine's Fables, decorate the seat and back of a sofa, the framework of which consists of richly carved and gilded wood. The ground, composed of the colour usually called Louis XV red, is cut out to the pattern of the carved wood, but plays only a secondary part, serving as an intermediary between the exterior gilding and the subject itself. This magnificent style of ornamentation belongs to the first part of the eighteenth century.

The specimen of binding with a pattern in gold on a green ground is by the younger Padeloup, one of the most skilful workmen of that period.

The two angles in carved wood were designed for the ceremony of the Coronation of Louis XV, which took place in 1722. They were executed by the Sieurs d'Ulin, of the Royal Academy of Painting and Sculpture, and Perrot, the Court-Painter. The mouldings and brackets belong to the same period. The Vitruvian scroll, adorned with fleurs de lys, is an example of the method of enrichment adopted by the ornamentalists of that time.

Launay, lith.

Imp Firmin-Didot fr Fils. & Cie Paris

XVIII CENTURY.

CARTOUCHES.

This plate terminates the series representing the different phases of the cartouche, the general characteristics of which we have already defined.

Nº 1.

Is from a service-book painted at Paris in 1740 for the church of St Gervais; it forms the framework of a blue camaïeu. (Mazarin Library. MS. 238 T.)

Nᵒˢ 2, 3.

These specimens are by Bernard Picart and also serve as frames to camaïeux.

The above three specimens, as well as Nᵒˢ 12 and 13, belong to the style of the close of the seventeenth century.

Nᵒˢ 4 to 7.

These subjects belong to a more equivocal style, viz to that excessive use of curves, which during a part of the century almost led to the abandonment of the straight line as an element of ornamentation.

Nº 8.

Stand in enamelled and painted earthenware.

Nº 9.

Book-plate painted in 1752 by Elias Nilson, director of the Academy of Augsburg, usually called the great Nilson.

Nᵒˢ 10, 11.

Emblematic cartouches, after De la Joue.

The four masks are by Abraham Bosse, and belong to the preceding century.

Nᵒˢ 2, 3, 8.

Specimens of damaskeening from 1720 to 1730.

Launay lith.　　　　　　　　　　　　　　　　　　Imp. Firmin Didot. fr. Fils & Cⁱᵉ, Paris.

XVIII CENTURY.

GOLDSMITHS' WORK, AND JEWELLERY.

Some of the clasps, called châtelaines, with which this plate is filled, belong to the style which was in fashion from 1719 to 1745; a style encouraged by the Oppenords and Meissonier, and carried to such a length by Babel, the celebrated goldsmith; the others belong to a later time.

In Jewellery and the arts that depend on it, especially chasing, works were produced at this time which have not since been surpassed. The French school, by adopting the liberty of form which prevailed in the new Italian style, succeeded in giving it a peculiar character of lightness and grace.

Nᵒˢ 1, 2, 3, 4, 5, 6, 7, 8, 10, 11.

Chains by Gilles l'Égaré.
These belong to the style of decoration practised by the Bérains and Marots at the close of the seventeenth century and the commencement of the eighteenth.

Nᵒ 9.

Seal by Gilles l'Égaré. (Same style.)

Nᵒˢ 12 to 19.

An almost complete set of ladies' ornaments of the time of Louis XVI : principal clasp with watch and seals, clasps, pins and egrets of different dimensions for the dress and hair.

Each of the other clasps represents the type of as many sets, composed of similar pieces, either for gentlemen or ladies.

Lith par F Durin. Imp. Firmin Didot fr. Fils & Cie Paris.

XVIII CENTURY.

PATTERNS OF SILKS.

HANGINGS FOR WALLS AND FURNITURE : CLOTHING.

The silks, the designs for which form the subject of our plate, all come from that branch of French manufacture to which Colbert, under Louis XIV, gave so powerful an impulse, and the productions of which, thanks to careful academical studies, and the wholesome traditions of the studios, have never ceased to influence all the European manufactories engaged in the production of these fabrics.

The twelve examples given in the accompanying plate may be classified in the following order. To this classification we have added a scale showing the relative proportion of each to the original.

	Nos	1	reduced to $\frac{1}{5}$
1o Hangings for furniture and walls. — State robes............................		2	— »
		3	— $\frac{1}{6}$
		4	— »
		5	— »
		6	— $\frac{1}{5}$
2o Idem, in two colours (Louis XVI).....................................		7	— »
		8	— »
		9	— »
3o Light silks (Louis XVI).....................................		10	— $\frac{1}{3}$
		11	— »
4o Border (Louis XVI).....................................		12	— »

In the first four of these, traces of the influence of Asiatic art on the national taste may be observed.

Numbers 3 and 4 deserve special attention from the manner in which by means of reflected rays richness and fulness are imparted to the primary simple designs.

Lastly, as a peculiarity in the process of manufacture, we notice in Nos 2, 3, 4, 10, 11, the use of silks figured with zonal patterns.

Lithographié par Painlevé.

Imp. Firmin-Didot fr. Fils & Cie Paris.

XVIII CENTURY.

SECOND PERIOD.

CHASING, ENAMELS, AND PAINTINGS.

Nº 1.

FAN.

(1750 to 1760.)

This fan, now in the possession of M. Alfred Firmin Didot, is particularly remarkable for the delicacy of its workmanship, which is such, that although formed of numerous very minute plate of ivory and mother-of-pearl lying one over the other, the design is uninterrupted and perfectly expressed.

The work bears much resemblance to the style of the engraver Babel, and it is believed to have come from his *atelier*.

Nᵒˢ 2, 3, 4.

SNUFF BOX.

Front, back, and sides.

1769.

This chased and enamelled gold box is the work of the celebrated goldsmith Auguste Laterre.

Collection of M. Léopold Double.

Nᵒˢ 5, 6, 7.

SNUFF BOX.

Front, back, and sides.

1780.

The chasing on this box is a master-piece of Mathis de Beaulieu, goldsmith to Louis XVI; it serves as a mounting to one of Petitot's most wonderful enamels, representing the portrait of Turenne, which has here been merely sketched in the place occupied by the original.

Collection of M. Léopold Double.

Nᵒˢ 8, 9, 10.

SNUFF BOXES.

1780 to 1790.

Collection of M. Leclercq, dealer in curiosities, Paris.

These enamelled gold boxes are ornamented with paintings in camaïeu.

Nᵒˢ 11, 12, 13, 14.

BORDERS AFTER DENEUFFORGE.

It is interesting to observe with the dates the changes in French taste during the latter half of the eighteenth century, changes which were in a great degree caused by the discovery of Pompeii and Herculaneum, so well suited to lead back to better principles the always ingenious but sometimes affected and involved manner of French artists.

Lith. par F. Durin.

Imp. Firmin-Didot fr. Fils & Cie, Paris.

XVIII CENTURY.

TAPESTRIES AND DAMASKEENINGS.

The specimens which occupy N°s 1 to 8 belong to the first part of the eighteenth century, and were publishep at that time by Mariette.

N° 9, belonging to the same time, is taken from Bernard Picart.

N° 10, is a panel in tapestry of the second part of the century, communicated by M. Leclercq, dealer in curiosities, Paris.

N°s 11 and 12, form a single pattern; copied from tapestry bed-hangings of the close of the eighteenth century, belonging to M. Léopold Double.

We must again remark here, as at plate (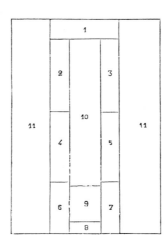), the difference in the ornamentation affected at the beginning of the century, from that which prevailed at its close, a difference due to the important fact of the discovery of Herculaneum and Pompeii.

Lith par Launey

Imp. Firmin-Didot fr. Fils & Cⁱᵉ Paris

XVIII CENTURY.

PAINTINGS ON PORCELAIN.

It was only in 1769, and after many failures, that the chemist Macquer, of Sèvres, was able to read to the Academy a complete memoir on hard French porcelain, and to exhibit some perfect specimens of it. Afterwards this manufacture was greatly developed under the management of Brongniart. The rage for translucid paintings thus obtained caused the production of an incalculable number, the principal types of which are given in our plate. They were named after the great personages for whom they were designed, and are known as the Porcelain of the Queen, of the Comte de Provence, of the Comte d'Artois, of the Duc d'Orléans, etc.

All these specimens are from the admirable collection of M. Léopold Double.

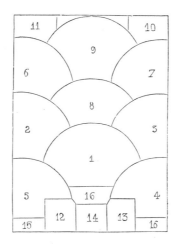

N° 1.

Plate forming part of a service, called the « Birds of Buffon, » which the illustrious author of the *Natural History* called his *Sèvres edition*, and which contains no fewer than 100 pieces, representing all the birds described in the book.

N°s 2 to 5.

N° 5 has the initials of Mme Dubarry.

N°s 6 to 9.

Specimens of different services.

N°s 10, 11.

Ornamental corners of trays.

N°s 12, 13.

Ground-work of trays.

N°s 14 to 16.

Open-worked borders of trays.

Lith par Launay.

Imp.Firmin-Didot fr. Fils & Cie Paris

XVIII CENTURY.

TROPHIES AND BOUQUETS.

The three subjects on a gold ground are pastoral trophies painted and varnished according to a process much in vogue during the last century, and of which we find the following account in a contemporary author :

« By means of processes resembling those of the Chinese and Japanese, the celebrated Martin, varnisher to the king, produced various kinds of card vases and snuff-boxes, which were much in fashion and repute in 1745; but, as the manufacture was not difficult, Paris, six years later, was perfectly inundated by imitators of this style who, seeking to injure one another, reduced the prices almost to nothing. Martin alone and his brothers retained their popularity, as they were masters of the art of repairing old Japan lackered ware, an accomplishment far superior to that of varnishing carriages and inventing snuff-boxes of mother of pearl. »

(*L'Art du peintre, doreur et vernisseur,* by the Sieur Watin, Paris, 1776).

The Martin varnishes are very rare, and have retained their high reputation. One of the specimens in our plate bears the initials of Marie-Antoinette. All the three are taken from a piece of furniture in the fine collection of M. Léopold Double.

The four specimens in grisaille are taken from panels, in which they represent the four seasons. The freedom and studied sobriety of these compositions appear to us to deserve attention.

The vase of flowers and ornamental leaves, occupying the centre of our plate, and signed with the name of Carlle, belongs to that modified style of decoration, which after the exhumation of Pompei characterized the Louis XVI period.

XVIII CENTURY.

DECORATIVE PAINTINGS.

This charming decoration is by the hand of Van Spaendonk, a celebrated Dutch painter established in France. He was born at Tilburg March 23rd 1746, and died at Paris May 11th 1822.

« The works of this painter, says the *Biographie Générale* (Didot 1855), are particularly distinguished for the excellence of their composition. The artist represents with the greatest accuracy the bloom on fruit, and the form and aspect of flowers; his colouring is fine, light, transparent, and full of freshness and harmony. »

These qualities may be noticed to a high degree in the panel here represented.

These paintings were ordered of the artist by the Comte d'Artois for *la Duthé*. The mansion they adorned in the *quartier* of the Chaussée-d'Antin, since become the hôtel Talabot, having been demolished, they were acquired by M. Léopold Double who has employed them in the decoration of a boudoir in his house in the Rue Louis le Grand, and it is by his kindness that we are able to place them before our readers.

Lith. par Launay.   Imp.Firmin-Didot fr Fils & Cie Paris